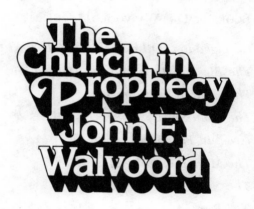

The
Church in
Prophecy
John F.
Walvoord

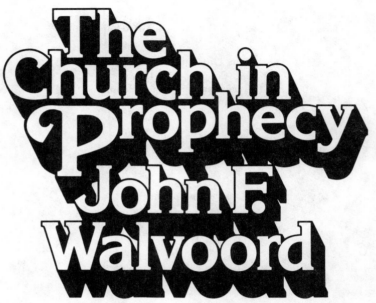

The Church in Prophecy

John F. Walvoord

President, Dallas Theological Seminary

ZONDERVAN PUBLISHING HOUSE

OF THE ZONDERVAN CORPORATION
GRAND RAPIDS, MICHIGAN 49506

THE CHURCH IN PROPHECY
Copyright 1964 by
Zondervan Publishing House
Grand Rapids, Michigan

Seventeenth printing 1981

Library of Congress Catalog Card No. 64-11955
ISBN 0-310-34051-9

Printed in the United States of America

CONTENTS

PREFACE

This study embodies a series of lectures on the subject of the church in prophecy delivered to the Grace College and Theological Seminary in Winona Lake, Indiana, in April 1963. Some of the lectures were delivered to the entire student body, others to the Seminary only, and one (Chapter VII) was given only to the faculty. Due to this peculiar circumstance, some repetition which occurred in the original presentation was allowed to stand in the editing. Because of limitation in the number of the lectures themselves, it seemed best to add several introductory chapters not included in the lecture series. As a whole the presentation is intended to provide a general study of prophecy as it relates to the church and as far as practical is couched in nontechnical language and with no attempt at documentation.

When Christ declared in His famous conversation with Peter, "I will build my church" (Matthew 16:18), He revealed one of the most important reasons for the incarnation. Christ had come to reveal God, to present Himself to Israel as their King, to die on the cross as our Redeemer, and to be raised from the dead in triumph; but undergirding the whole was the divine purpose to found the church as the supreme example of the grace of God in time and eternity (Ephesians 2:5-10).

Because of the central place of the doctrine of the church in the New Testament, it has occupied the minds of intelligent students of the Word of God from the beginning of Christianity. The church introduced in the Gospels and revealed in its intrinsic character in the Upper Room Discourse (John 13-17) is found in action in the book of Acts. Its theology, ethics, polity, and prophetic hope are unfolded in the epistles. Its consummation is described in the book of the Revelation.

In that the purpose of God from the foundation of the world for the church was eschatological in its essence, it is only natural that the subject of prophecy as it relates to the church should be a prominent feature of Christian theology. The Biblical purity of the hope of the church has been unfortunately obscured by basic differences of opinion on the literalness of the Scriptural promises and prophetic program set forth in the New Testament. This has complicated the study of this aspect of Biblical truth and has resulted in prophecy being neglected in much of the scholarly literature of our day. Because of the diversity of interpretation of prophecy, any treatment is inevitably controversial as no approach will satisfy any considerable majority of Christian scholars.

The presentation of this study of prophecy as it relates to the church has certain presuppositions. The Bible is considered to be the final court of appeal and its words are regarded as infallibly inspired of God. In the interpretation of prophecy, the same general principles of exposition of the Word of God are followed as in other areas of theology, namely, the normal or literal meaning of the words is assumed unless good ground is discovered for another meaning. The church is regarded as the body of believers of the present age as distinguished from the saints of the Old Testament, the nation Israel, or saints of future ages. Two major aspects of the church are distinguished, namely, the body of Christ composed of all true believers in the present age, and the professing church or Christendom, formed by all who are included in the organized church in its largest dimension. Their respective prophetic programs, though largely parallel, now have a sharply different consummation. The view is defended that the hope of the church is vital to any true believer in Christ, being important theologically and practically, as well as eschatologically. Ours is indeed "that blessed hope, and the glorious appearing of the great God and our Saviour Jesus Christ" (Titus 2:13).

If the evidences accumulating in our generation are properly understood to be indications that the end of the age is at hand, the prophecies expounded in this volume are more than theological facts. They are a thrilling anticipation of that which even now may be impending upon the people of God. Though not intended to be exhaustive, these expositions nevertheless provide a panorama of future events which constitute the heritage of the child of God and the hope of every believer in Christ. The great truths delineated here are held with deep conviction. While tempered by the obvious fact that "now we see through a glass darkly," our hope is nevertheless radiant with the prospect of seeing our Lord "face to face" (I Corinthians 13:12), with the hope of realization of all that which we now imperfectly understand. If students of the Word find in these pages enrichment of hope and increased understanding of the divine program of God for His own, the author will be deeply gratified.

JOHN F. WALVOORD

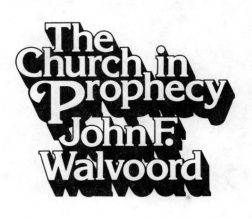

The
Church in
Prophecy

John F.
Walvoord

Chapter I

THE CHURCH IN THE OLD TESTAMENT

The Promise of a Seed

When Adam buried Abel after he was murdered by his brother Cain, it must have seemed that all hope was dead. Adam and Eve had enjoyed the marvelous experience of a life in perfect fellowship with God unmarred by sin. Then had come temptation, the act of disobedience, and the experience of evil. In the wreckage of what they once had been, as created by God, Adam and Eve heard the solemn words of divine judgment. They were now under a severe curse. Sorrow, pain, and struggle were to be their portion, and ultimately the dust of the earth was to reclaim their bodies. But there had been one ray of light. God had predicted that the woman would have a son, and that from his descendants One would come who would bruise the head of the serpent (Genesis 3:15). In anticipation of this, "Adam called his wife's name Eve; because she was the mother of all living" (Genesis 3:20).

In keeping with this promise, Cain and then Abel were born in due time, and the prospect of ultimate redemption from sin seemed to rest in one of these two young and active boys. As they grew up, it became evident that God's blessing was in a special way upon Abel. But now Abel was dead, and how could God use Cain, the murderer, to fulfill His purpose of redemption?

It was in this context of sin and divine judgment that another son was born whose name was Seth. The Hebrew name means "appointed," and Adam and Eve accepted the little child in place of Abel. As he grew up, it became more evident that God's purpose for fulfillment of the promise was to rest in Seth and his posterity, and a post-script appended to the record of the birth of a son to Seth revealed that "then began men to call upon the name of the LORD" (Genesis 4:26).

The purpose of God not only to provide a Redeemer but also a testimony to His name through a godly seed gradually unfolds in the Old Testament. It soon became evident that the great mass of humanity would not honor God. In the words of Genesis 6:5, "God saw that the wickedness of man was great in the earth, and that every imagination of the thoughts of his heart was only evil continually." As a result, God announced His purpose to destroy the race by a great flood and instructed Noah to prepare for it by building an ark for himself and his family. Once again, God was starting over with a godly seed.

The new beginning, however, did not result in any better situation than that of the civilization prior to the flood. The eleventh chapter of Genesis records the rebellion of men as they attempted to build a tower into the heavens. The divine history of the Old Testament now reveals a new divine purpose. In His selection of Abraham and his seed, God undertook to fulfill the promise of a Redeemer as well as to provide a continuing channel of testimony to the world in a nation to come from Abraham's descendants.

THE PROMISE OF A NATION

In the covenant given to Abraham in Genesis 12:1-3, God not only promised to make Abraham great and to provide through him the Messiah who was to be a blessing to all nations of the earth, but He made the pronouncement, "And I will make of thee a great nation." To this nation God promised perpetuity in an everlasting covenant (Genesis 17:7), and gave the perpetual title to the land of Canaan defined in Genesis 15:18 as extending from the River of Egypt unto the River Euphrates. This was to be an everlasting covenant as indicated in the words: "And I will give unto thee, and to thy seed after thee, the land wherein thou art a stranger, all the land of Canaan, for an everlasting possession; and I will be their God" (Genesis 17:8).

The promise of a great nation was ultimately fulfilled in the birth of Isaac, Jacob, the twelve patriarchs, and their posterity. The blessing pronounced upon Rebekah and the prayer that she should be the mother "of thousands of millions" perhaps not yet been literally fulfilled (Genesis 24:60), but the children of Israel have indeed become beyond enumeration as the dust of the earth and the stars of the heavens. In spite of many attempts to exterminate them and blot them from the face of the earth as recorded in Scripture as well as in the history of our modern era, the children of Israel have continued to this hour with more than two million of them now established in their new state of Israel.

The purpose of God in Israel is evident from the Scriptures themselves. Through Israel God was to have a testimony to the world concerning His sovereignty, His righteousness, His faithfulness, and His love. Israel was the object lesson both of the grace of God and His righteous judgment. Through the prophets of Israel came the voice of God to a people who needed to know Him. From the pens of Israelites flowed the Holy Scriptures. The moral law contained in the law of Moses as well as the religious system which it set up instituted a revelation of divine truth which has rewarded richly all who have studied it.

THE PROMISE OF THE KINGDOM

Among the wonderful prophecies unfolding God's purpose were the promises of God to the nation Israel containing predictions of a future kingdom. This is anticipated in the promise to Abraham that "kings should come out of thee" (Genesis 17:6). The line of the promised king is narrowed to the tribe of Judah in Genesis 49:10, and subsequently is outlined in detail to David in God's covenant with him (II Samuel 7:12-16). David is promised that his physical posterity would continue forever and that one of his seed would sit on the Davidic throne forever (II Samuel 7:16). Conservative scholarship agrees that this promise is fulfilled in Christ. Premillenarians generally accept the interpretation that this will be fulfilled in Christ's millennial reign on earth in keeping with the concept that it is a Davidic throne rather than a heavenly throne that is in view.

The promise given to David is subsequently enlarged in many other portions of Scripture (I Chronicles 17:4-27; Psalm 89:20-37) and becomes an important part of the future of Israel as a nation when they are regathered from the ends of the earth and brought back to their ancient land. At that time they will be ruled by a king described as fulfilling the promise: "Behold, the day is come, saith the LORD, that I will raise unto David a righteous Branch, and a King shall reign and prosper, and shall execute judgment and justice in the earth. In his days Judah will be saved, and Israel shall dwell safely: and this is his name whereby he shall be called, THE LORD OUR RIGHTEOUSNESS" (Jeremiah 23:5, 6).

The Old Testament as a whole is not only a remarkable record of prophecy itself but also contains the literal fulfillment of many of these promises. God's promises to Adam and Eve and their posterity were largely fulfilled in the subsequent history of the race. The promise to Abraham was realized through the nation Israel, though the ultimate possession of the land and the restoration of Israel are unfulfilled as the Old Testament closes. The prediction of an everlasting kingdom to David, though not fulfilled in the Old Testament, is confirmed by the birth of Christ and the announcement to Mary that her Son would reign over the house of Israel (Luke 1:31-33). If interpreted literally, the promises of the Old Testament assure a future restoration of Israel and a future kingdom of David in the millennial period.

A point of view typical of amillenarianism is to regard these prophecies in a nonliteral sense. By some, the nation Israel is considered to be an early stage of the church and organically one with the church of the New Testament. Likewise, the promises addressed to David concerning his future are spiritualized to represent divine government over the earth such as is true in the present age. This point of view has also supported the concepts that the church in the Old Testament is essentially one with the church of the New Testament. Premillenarians who interpret prophecy literally, rather than figuratively, tend to distinguish believers in Christ in the present age from the saints of Old Testament. It is important in attempting to understand these various points of view to recognize both points of agreement and points of disagreement.

All agree that the Old Testament records promises to Israel, some of which are fulfilled in the Old Testament. Some disagreement exists concerning how these prophecies are to be fulfilled in the future. All agree that there are saints in the Old Testament, that is, a body of believers whose sins are forgiven and who will have a blessed eternity in the presence of God. Disagreement exists as to whether the term church is properly applied to these saints of the Old Testament. Many times it is taken for granted that if there are saints in the Old Testament they belong to the universal church.

A careful study of both the Old and New Testament, however, seems to justify the conclusion that something new began on the Day of Pentecost, namely, a body of believers distinct in divine purpose and situation from saints who preceded them in the Old Testament. The New Testament word for *church, ekklesia,* is a common Greek word which has a long history. It was originally used to describe the assembly of Greek citizens. The word comes from the verb *ekkaleo* meaning "to call out," but its usage seems to emphasize the resultant meaning of being called out, namely, an assembly or gathering of a people for some purpose. It is in this sense that it is used many times in the New Testament.

The Greek word *ekklesia* was used in a Greek translation of the Old Testament known as the Septuagint, which was in common use during the first century A.D. Though many different Hebrew words have the idea of assembly or congregation, only one of them, the Hebrew word *qahal*, was translated *ekklesia*. The use of *ekklesia* in seventy-seven passages in the Old Testament has been cited by some as proof sufficient that the church in a religious sense is found in the Old Testament.

An examination of these passages demonstrates, however, that *qahal*, when translated *ekklesia*, is always used in reference to an assembly or meeting of some description in one locality, i.e., a physical assembly, and the word is never used to represent the idea of a mystic company of saints joined in a spiritual way, though scattered geographically. The idea of the church as an *ekklesia* composed of individual saints widely scattered geographically is never found in the Old Testament. Though Israel was in some sense a spiritual community, its character was principally racial and political rather than a spiritual entity. While the term, "the seed of Abraham," is used in Galatians 3: 6-9 to represent anyone, either Jew or Gentile, who follows Abram's example of faith in God, the term, *Israel,* or *Jew* or *seed of Israel,* is never used to include Gentile believers. These terms, therefore, are not equivalent to the idea of the church. Though the concept of a church in the Old Testament in the sense of a spiritual community is a common idea in theology, it has no support in the terminology used in the Old Testament itself. The use of *ekklesia* as a term describing the body of Christ, i.e., all believers in the present age both in earth and heaven, is peculiar to the New Testament and signified a new undertaking of God divorced from His program for Israel and for Gentiles which was revealed in the Old Testament history and prophecy.

The fact that there were saints in the Old Testament demonstrates the underlying redemptive purpose of God spanning the whole of human history and constitutes a unifying factor in the revelation of divine love and redemptive purpose. But the concept of the church as it is unfolded in the New Testament is dramatically different and is an important division of the over-all work of God in salvation.

The divine purpose of God for salvation as revealed in the Old Testament is therefore not synonymous with God's purpose for the seed of Abraham, the nation of Israel, nor the Davidic kingdom. These divine purposes will have their ultimate fulfillment which will involve saints. But these programs are not God's redemptive purpose specifically. Prophecy as it relates to the church is, therefore, a different subject having a different program and having factors which are foreign to God's program for either Jews or Gentiles as contained in Old Testament revelation.

The Old Testament forms an important background and setting for the incarnation, and Christ came to earth to fulfill the promise of the coming seed of the woman which would bruise the head of the serpent. Christ was indeed the Son of Abraham who would bring blessing to all nations. Christ came also as the Son of David who was qualified to sit upon the Davidic throne. Christ came in His first advent to provide salvation through His death and resurrection for all who believe in Him. In His second and yet future coming, He will fulfill His role as the Son of David and deliverer of the nation Israel. Between the first and second coming of Christ, the pronouncement He made, "I will build my church" (Matthew 16:18), will be fulfilled. Prophecy, as it relates to the church, is therefore concerned with the fulfillment of this prediction rather than those relating to the nation Israel or to the kingdom promised to David.

Chapter II

THE CHURCH AS THE NEW TESTAMENT ASSEMBLY

Major Concepts of the Church

The Old Testament ended with the major prophecies relating to Israel and the world as a whole unfulfilled. The most important factor was lacking, namely, the fulfillment of the prophecies concerning the coming Messiah. With the coming of Christ as recorded in the New Testament, a new order is introduced, recognized by the very title, "The New Testament." Though in a large measure it constituted a fulfillment of that which was anticipated in the Old Testament, it soon became evident that much was now to be revealed which formerly was hidden.

The Gospel of Matthew especially traces this important transition. Christ, who is introduced as the King of Israel, of the line of David, and of the seed of Abraham, is rejected by His own people. The ethical principles of His kingdom outlined in Matthew 5-7 do not capture the interest or faith of the majority of the nation and especially its leaders. The miracles which Christ performed, which were the prophesied credentials of the Messiah, are rejected, and Christ is accused of performing His miracles by the power of the devil (Matthew 12:24).

In the face of such rejection, Christ pronounces a solemn judgment upon His generation, and His message turns from that of presentation of Himself as the Messiah of Israel to one of invitation to personal discipleship as illustrated in Matthew 11:28-30. In Matthew 13, the rejection of Christ is anticipated and the period between

20

His first and second advent is made the subject of prophecy. After further evidence of rejection on the part of His people, a dynamic new proclamation is revealed in connection with Peter's confession of faith, recorded in Matthew 16:16, "Thou art the Christ, the Son of the living God." In reply, Christ says: "Blessed art thou, Simon Bar-jona: for flesh and blood hath not revealed it unto thee, but my Father which is in heaven. And I say also unto thee, That thou art Peter, and upon this rock I will build my church; and the gates of hell shall not prevail against it" (Matthew 16: 17, 18).

Of major significance is the declaration, "I will build my church." What is here contemplated is obviously not a continuation of that which had begun in the Old Testament. Christ did not say, "I will redeem Israel," or, "I will proclaim my salvation to the Gentiles." Rather, in the face of national rejection on the part of Israel, He proclaims a new divine purpose, namely the formation of a new assembly to be delineated on spiritual rather than racial lines and without territorial or political characteristics. It was to be composed of those who, like Peter, had confessed Jesus Christ as the Son of God.

A wide variety of opinion has arisen concerning the exact meaning of this dramatic pronouncement. All agree that the church is part of the plan of God for salvation of the elect. Some hold that the church is only a continued development of the plan of God for Israel in the New Testament and try to identify the church with Israel. Others consider it a phase of fulfillment of God's covenant purpose relating to salvation. Still others regard it as an aspect of the over-all kingdom of God of which the church is a segment. There are also those who combine various aspects of these ideas.

Much of the confusion that exists in the doctrine of the church has resulted from contrasting too sharply the various viewpoints. There are elements of truth in each approach. What is adopted for this discussion is the view that the church which Christ stated He would build is indeed an aspect of God's general program of salvation, but that this program in many respects is distinct from the Old Testament revelation and is not a fulfillment of God's plan and purpose for the nation of Israel. Further, the purpose of Christ for the church is not a realization of the kingdom promises of the Old Testament which will be fulfilled in the future millennium following Christ's advent. The support for this point of view is found in the details revealed in the New Testament concerning the church as the body of Christ. These will be unfolded in later discussion.

THE DAY OF PENTECOST

Most expositors agree that the New Testament church in some sense began on the Day of Pentecost. Though Christ anticipated a new fellowship and a new selective testimony for God, He did not bring into being a genuine fulfillment of the prophecy that He would build His church. The church could not be properly begun until after His death and resurrection and the coming of the Spirit.

On the Day of Pentecost, the prophecy of Christ that they would be baptized by the Spirit "not many days hence" (Acts 1:5) was fulfilled and with this the New Testament church formally began. The Apostle Peter later referred to this as "at the beginning" (Acts 11:15), when the Lord's prophecy of the baptism of the Spirit was fulfilled (Acts 11:16). Not only were they baptized with the Spirit, but as Acts 2:4 testified, "They were all filled with the Holy Ghost." With the advent of the Spirit, three thousand souls were added (Acts 2:41), and the body of believers from then on was characterized as the church. There now was a genuine New Testament assembly, as most Christian scholars recognize in some form.

The apostolic church could be distinguished as having two major aspects: (1) its outer testimony as a body of professed followers of the Lord Jesus Christ, and (2) the spiritual church composed of all true believers and referred to as "the body of Christ" (I Corinthians 12:13, 27). The distinction is one of a sphere of profession in contrast to a sphere of reality, the outward in contrast to the inward, the geographic or local in contrast to the universal. Though there has been confusion and disagreement on this distinction, it seems to be a justifiable concept, and is recognized to some extent by all branches of Christendom. From the standpoint of prophecy, it is important that the two entities be distinguished.

The New Testament has much teaching concerning the church as a local assembly. The body of believers originally formed in Jerusalem was soon duplicated in smaller measure elsewhere. Reference is made in Scripture to "the church which was at Jerusalem" (Acts 1:8); "the church which is at Cenchrea" (Romans 16:1); "the church of God which is at Corinth" (I Corinthians 1:2); and the New Testament contains many similar references. Sometimes the word church is used as a plural, a clear reference to a local assembly as in Acts 15:41 and Romans 16:16. It sometimes had a geographic designation as a reference to "the churches of Galatia" (Galatians 1:2), i.e., the churches located in the area of Galatia. The concept of local churches as in contrast to the church of the body of Christ, which is always in the singular, is consistently observed in the New Testament.

In some instances, however, the professing church seems to be referred to in the Bible without reference to locality, as illustrated in Romans 16:16, "the churches of Christ" (cp. I Corinthians 15:9; Philippians 3:6). These could, however, be interpreted as references either to local assemblies when in the plural or to the body of Christ when in the singular. The mention of the church in Galatia (Galatians 1:13; cp. Philippians 3:6) may well be taken as referring to the professing church in general. The many instances where the church is mentioned in its outer geographic character justifies the concept of the gradual formation of the New Testament assembly composed of local

congregations which included not only true Christians but
those who professed to follow Christ. That these local congregations cannot be equated with the body of Christ is
evident from such passages as Revelation 3:14-19 where the
church of Laodicea obviously includes those who are not
regenerated. Thus in apostolic days arose the early organized church which later developed into the far-flung body
of professed believers which constitutes Christendom in its
largest dimension.

One of the important themes of prophecy in the New
Testament is that pertaining to the course of the present
age. Many of these prophecies relate to the organized
church, in contrast to prophecies that relate to the body of
Christ. The course of the age in general is developed under
the prophetic theme of the kingdom of heaven revealed in
Matthew 13 with other Scriptures, such as Matthew 24,
I Timothy 4, II Timothy 2, 3, and Revelation 17, describing the trend toward apostasy which will have its climax
in the future great tribulation. The course of the professing
church extends from the first coming of Christ to His second
coming to the earth and is a broader revelation than that
relating to the body of Christ which properly began on the
Day of Pentecost and culminates in the translation of the
true church before the professing church comes to its end.

THE COURSE OF THE CHURCH IN THE PRESENT AGE

The relationship of the kingdom of heaven to the church
is one of the difficult areas of Biblical interpretation. Some
have equated the kingdom idea with the church for all
practical purposes, and others have attempted sharp distinction. Generally speaking, however, a distinction may
be observed between God's general government over the
world and God's particular rule over the saints. In contrast to both of these ideas is the prophesied kingdom of
the Old Testament in which Christ will rule on earth and
bring in a kingdom of perfect righteousness, justice, and
peace. It is this earthly, Messianic kingdom which is given

prominence in the Old Testament and which will find fulfillment after the second coming of Christ according to Revelation 20. The kingdom on earth, while obviously having
spiritual characteristics and constituting a major aspect of
the delivering and saving work of God, is essentially political and theocratic. It was this Messianic kingdom which
was announced at hand in connection with the coming of
Christ, and it was this kingdom that was rejected when
Christ was rejected.

A basic cleavage in the interpretation of prophecy over
the doctrine of the kingdom is found in comparing the
amillennial and premillennial interpretations. Amillenarians generally hold that the kingdom of the Old Testament
is realized in the church in the present age, whereas premillenarians view the kingdom as future and following the
second coming of Christ. If the premillennial interpretation be adopted, it still leaves some important decisions
for the interpreter of Scripture, and one of these areas is
in relation to the kingdom of heaven in Matthew 13.

In Matthew, chapter 13, a series of parables is used
by our Lord to unfold the mysteries of the kingdom of
heaven. The expression, "kingdom of heaven," which is
peculiar to the Gospel of Matthew has been usually considered identical to a similar expression in the other gospels, "the kingdom of God." In many respects, the two ex-
pressions seem to be the same, as the term *heaven* is a
Hebraism for God.

In some instances, however, there seems to be a contrast
between the kingdom of heaven as it is portrayed in Matthew's Gospel and the kingdom of God as it is unfolded
in the other Gospels and the rest of the New Testament.
This distinction in its simplest form is a contrast between
the kingdom of God, viewed as containing all saints and
excluding those not regenerated, and the kingdom of heaven
as a sphere of profession, which includes those who are
outwardly related to Christ but not actually to be numbered
with the saints. If the kingdom of God be viewed as God's

universal government, it of course would include all these, but when it is used in the sense of containing only the saved and as requiring new birth to enter (John 3:5), then the kingdom of heaven is the broader term and is so used in Matthew 13. This distinction, though helpful, is largely an exegetical one which does not affect either the doctrine of the church or prophecy as a whole. A further distinction, however, can be observed between the kingdom in its present form, whether the kingdom of God or the kingdom of heaven, and the kingdom in its future or millennial form. It is this latter distinction between the present and future forms of the kingdom in which prophecy comes to the fore.

It is a major error to make the word *kingdom,* which is a common term, always mean the same in all its uses. Rather, it must be interpreted by its context. Outside the Gospel of Matthew, however, the kingdom of God is used in the New Testament only to refer to God's spiritual kingdom or His governmental kingdom. Only in Matthew and in the terminology of "the kingdom of heaven" is the concept of a sphere of a profession presented. It is for this reason that Matthew 13 assumes major proportions in an attempt to understand God's prophetic program for the professing church.

The term, "kingdom of God," is never in Scripture made a synonym of the church either as the body of Christ or as a sphere of profession. Because it refers to the same time period, i.e., the interadvent period, and because it relates to the same spiritual and moral problems, however, it does reveal spiritual truth which characterizes the present age. Hence, the parables of Matthew 13, though related to the mysteries of the kingdom of heaven, also constitute a revelation of the progress of the professing church in the period between the first and second advent.

In understanding the mysteries of the kingdom of heaven, it is most significant that they are introduced as "mysteries." This term is properly used throughout the New

Testament to describe truth revealed in the New Testament which was hidden from view as far as Old Testament revelation is concerned. It is specifically New Testament truth. The truths contained in the mysteries of the kingdom, therefore, are not an exposition of the Old Testament doctrine of the kingdom as it will be fulfilled in the millennium, but rather a presentation of truth as it relates to the kingdom in the present age. In contrast to the millennial period, when the kingdom will be visible and the King will be on earth, the present age features the King's absence and the rule of His subjects by invisible and spiritual means only.

In attempting to understand the seven parables of Matthew 13 as they constitute prophecy of the church in the present age, it is most important to observe that the first two parables are interpreted by Christ Himself. By using this key, the other parables also can be understood.

The seven parables were expounded by Christ as He sat in the ship just off the shore of the Sea of Galilee with a multitude on the bank to hear His proclamation. The first parable was suited for such a situation, relating the parable of the sower casting seed on various kinds of soil. As interpreted by Christ, the good news of the kingdom is received in various ways. Some seed falls on the hard-beaten wayside which is totally unreceptive and is carried away by the fowls without bearing fruit. Other seed falls upon places where the soil is shallow and where its lack of depth does not provide room for the seed to root. This is related to those who eagerly hear the Word, but soon give it up when trial comes.

Two classes of believers are said to receive the Word with some effectiveness. One of these is characterized as having heard the Word, but the Word is described as becoming unfruitful because of the "cares of this world, and the deceitfulness of riches" (Matthew 13:22). The one who receives the seed in good soil and properly hears the Word brings forth fruit, "some an hundredfold, some sixty, some thirty" (Matthew 13:23). This parable, which relates to reception of the proclaimed Word, makes clear that the present age cannot be equated with the millennium when all will be forced to obey Christ and make at least an outward profession of faith in Him. Here a picture of the present age is given. Just as the word of the kingdom in Christ's day was rarely received by more than a few, so the word of truth in the present age will seldom fall on good ground and only occasionally will come into soil where it will bring forth its hundredfold fruit. In the present age, only a fraction of those who hear the Gospel will come to Christ.

The second parable concerning the wheat and the tares brings out the same idea, but in a different figure. Here the seed sown represented in the wheat is the believer himself. Along with believers, however, described as children of the kingdom (Matthew 13:38), "tares" are sown, representing imitation wheat which grows with the good wheat until the harvest time. When the harvest occurs, the tares are gathered first and burned, but the wheat is gathered into the barn (Matthew 13:30). The truth presented in this parable is that when Christ comes to establish His kingdom on earth false profession will be judged and unbelievers destroyed. Only those who are true believers will be gathered into the kingdom. This judgment occurs when Christ comes to the earth after the great tribulation rather than at the rapture of the church when the tares are left undisturbed, according to the pretribulational interpretation.

The other parables, though left uninterpreted, contribute further elements to our understanding of the progress of the present age. The parable of the mustard seed (Matthew 13:31, 32) indicates the tremendous growth of the professing church from a small beginning, symbolized by the mustard seed, to its present tremendous proportions. History has certainly confirmed this interpretation as well as the details which are added, namely, that the birds of the air, representing Satan and those that he controls, will come and lodge in its branches.

The fourth parable recorded in Matthew 13:33-35 states, "The kingdom of heaven is like unto leaven, which a woman took, and hid in three measures of meal, till the whole was leavened." This illustration taken from common life refers to the practice of taking leaven or fermented dough and adding it to new dough in order to extend the leavening process. There has been some disagreement as to what the leaven signifies. In the postmillennial interpretation, the leaven has been likened to the Gospel which permeates the whole lump, referring to the whole world. While it is true that Christianity has had its effect upon the world as a whole, this interpretation seems to violate the usual use of leaven to represent that which is evil. In the Passover, unleavened bread had to be used because of this significance.

In the New Testament, leaven seems to symbolize externalism, worldliness, hypocrisy, and bad doctrine. It is unfortunately true that the professing church has all of these elements and if leaven was intended to signify evil, it has already been fulfilled. The same is the case even with the true church which has fallen far short of what it ought to have been. The optimism of the postmillennial view has largely been discarded today, and with the new realization of the power of evil, the interpretation of this parable should be brought into proper focus. Nowhere does the Bible picture the present age as one of gradual improvement. It is rather, as will be seen in the study of the doctrine of apostasy in the church, that evil represented in this parable as leaven will increase and the professing church eventually will be engulfed by it.

The fifth parable is presented in Matthew 13:44: "Again, the kingdom of heaven is like unto treasure hid in a field; the which when a man hath found, he hideth, and for joy thereof goeth and selleth all that he hath, and buyeth that field." This has often been taken as a parallel to the sixth parable of Matthew 13:45, 46 referring to the pearl:

"Again, the kingdom of heaven is like unto a merchant man, seeking goodly pearls: who, when he had found one pearl of great price, went and sold all that he had, and bought it."

What is the meaning of the treasure described as hidden in the field and the pearl described as of great price? A common interpretation has been that the treasure in the field and the pearl of great price are none other than Christ and that the man who finds the treasure and the merchant man who buys the pearl are a picture of the believer. This interpretation, however, disregards the theological context of our salvation, for a believer has nothing with which to buy Christ and, as a matter of fact, Christ is not for sale. Salvation rather originates in God and is God's free gift bestowed without regard to merit on the part of the recipient.

A better interpretation is that in these two parables is revealed the twofold aspect of the death of Christ, on the one hand redeeming Israel, signified by the treasure hid in the field, and on the other hand the redemptive purpose of Christ for the church, signified by the pearl of great price. Israel in spiritual significance is largely hidden in the world and yet is a treasure in the eyes of God (Exodus 19:5; Psalm 135:4). Christ in His death actually bought the whole world represented by "that field" but in the process redeemed Israel, the treasure hidden in the field. In like manner, the merchantman who buys the pearl of great price symbolizes Christ in His redemptive act on the cross. Just as a pearl is an outgrowth of an irritation in the side of the oyster, so the church in a symbolic sense is begotten in the wounds of Christ and is a precious jewel for which Christ gave all that He had. The two parables taken together, therefore, seem to reflect Christ's love for Israel and for His church. Both of these are, of course, illustrated in the present age as well as in the future purpose of God.

The concluding parable, that of the dragnet, is presented in Matthew 13:47-50, "Again, the kingdom of heaven is like unto a net, that was cast into the sea, and gathered of every kind: which, when it was full, they drew to shore, and sat down, and gathered the good into vessels, but cast the bad away. So shall it be at the end of the world: the angels shall come forth, and sever the wicked from among the just, and shall cast them into the furnace of fire: there shall be wailing and gnashing of teeth." Here again is dramatic proof that the present age is quite different from the millennium for the net gathers of every kind, both good and bad fish. The kingdom of heaven in this passage also stands in contrast to the kingdom of God in the other Gospels where the kingdom of God seems to be restricted to those who are born again. Here the kingdom of heaven includes the bad fish in the net as well as the good, and the Scriptures say specifically that the net "gathered of every kind" (Matthew 13:47).

The Scriptures make clear that this judgment will occur at the second coming of Christ "at the end of the world," or better translated, "at the end of the age." Just as the good and bad fish are separated, so here in Matthew 13:49, 50 the angel is seen putting the good into vessels, but casting the bad away, symbolic of the future judgment at the second coming of Christ when the righteous will go into the millennial kingdom and the wicked will be cast into the furnace of fire (cp. Matthew 25:41). The time when this will occur is at the end of the tribulation and at the beginning of the millennial kingdom when the sphere of profession is brought to a close in its present form.

As in the parable of the wheat and the tares, there is emphasis here on the dual line of development within the sphere of profession, namely, those that are true believers symbolized by the wheat and the good fish as contrasted to those who are merely professing believers who, though intermingled with the true believers now, will be separated from them at the end of the age. In contrast to the millennium when judgments will be inflicted immediately upon those that rebel against Christ, this is descriptive of the present age when God is withholding judgment and reserving it for the consummation.

The seven parables taken together therefore reveal that the general characteristics of the present age include the elements of a proclaimed message which will be only partially received. The parables show the intermingling of the saved with those who merely profess salvation, the rapid growth of the professing church to a great world-wide organization symbolized by the mustard seed, the permeation within the professing church as well as the true church symbolized by the leaven, the demonstration of the love of Christ both for Israel and the church symbolized in the purchase of the field with its treasure and the purchase of the pearl of great price, and finally the fact that the present age is subject to divine judgment when the saved will be separated from the unsaved as illustrated in the parable of the dragnet. Matthew 13, therefore, constitutes a comprehensive picture of the general features of the present age as distinguished from the Old Testament period in which Israel was in prominence and also in contrast to the millennial kingdom in which Christ will rule with a rod of iron.

THE PREDICTED TREND TOWARD APOSTASY

No notion was ever imposed upon the evangelical church with less justification than the postmillennial idea of gradual progress and ultimate spiritual triumph of the church. The idea that the Gospel would gradually subdue the people of the world and eventually bring them to the feet of Christ is contradicted alike both by the Scriptures and by history, and the result has been the rapid decline in the twentieth century of optimism in relation to the triumph of the church in the present age.

A survey of Scriptural prophecy as it relates to the spiritual trends of the present age should have made clear to any inquirer that the present age will end in apostasy and divine judgment rather than victory for the cause of Christ through the triumph of the church. Major passages of Scripture deal with this subject and the expositor is

embarrassed by the wealth of material which plainly teaches
that the end of the age will be characterized by apostasy
(Matthew 24:4-26; II Thessalonians 2:1-12; I Timothy 4:
1-3; II Timothy 3:1-9; 4:3, 4; II Peter 2:1 – 3:18; Jude 3-19;
Revelation 3:14-16; 6:1 – 19:21). An examination of these
major passages on apostasy in the New Testament will reveal that the development of apostasy will be in three
stages: (1) the doctrinal and moral departure in the church
prior to the rapture, i.e., during the last days of the true
church on earth; (2) the apostasy in the professing church
after the true church is raptured, i.e., in the period immediately following the rapture: (3) the final apostasy in
which the professing church as such will be destroyed and
the worship of the beast, the world ruler, as the human
representative of Satan will be inaugurated (Matthew 24:
15; II Thessalonians 2:3-12; Revelation 13:4-8; 17:16-18).
Of major importance is the fulfillment of the prophecy relating to apostasy in the church being fulfilled in the contemporary situation, a subject to which the Scriptures give
considerable space. Attention will be directed to prophecies related to the end of the age in later discussion.

Chapter III

THE CHURCH AS THE BODY OF CHRIST

The Announcement of the Divine Purpose

In the first mention of the church in the New Testament, a pronouncement was made by Christ Himself which is fundamental to the unfolding doctrine of the church as the body of Christ. In Matthew 16:15, Christ has asked His disciples, "But whom say ye that I am?" Simon Peter in response to this question answered, "Thou art the Christ, the Son of the living God" (Matthew 16:16). In commenting on this confession of faith in which Peter spoke representing the disciples, Jesus replied: "Blessed art thou, Simon Bar-jona: for flesh and blood hath not revealed it unto thee, but my Father which is in heaven. And I say also unto thee, That thou art Peter, and upon this rock I will build my church; and the gates of hell shall not prevail against it" (Matthew 16:17, 18).

The enigmatic statement of Christ in verse 18 has been the subject of much discussion. The Roman Church has taken the position that Christ was affirming that the church would be built upon Peter as the first pope. Protestants generally have rejected this interpretation, some holding that Christ meant that the church would be built upon the confession of faith of Christ as made by Peter, and others that the reference to "this rock" was a reference to Christ Himself. There is evidently a play on words in verse 18 as the reference to Peter in the Greek is *petros* which, while referring to Peter, has also the meaning of a "little rock." The reference to "this rock" uses a similar word, *petra*. Translated literally it would be, "Thou art Little Rock, and

upon this rock I will build my church." The resultant meaning is that Peter as a believer in Christ is a little rock, but
that the church as a whole must be built upon Christ, the
rock, as Peter himself is most careful to point out (I Peter
2:4-8).

From the standpoint of the doctrine of the church itself, the importance of this statement is in its sharp contrast
with the divine purpose in the Old Testament as related
to Israel and the nations, and God's present purpose here
announced by Christ Himself in the statement, "I will build
my church." Each word of this pronouncement is freighted
with meaning.

Christ, first of all, makes clear that the church to which
He is referring is something which is built by God rather
than by man. It is a sovereign undertaking by divine om-
nipotence, not a building to be erected by human hands.
The tense of the verb is future and the statement, therefore, constitutes a prophecy of things to come. Christ did
not say, "I am building my church," which would imply
that He had already begun the church, which, perhaps, would
justify the idea that the church is a continuation of what God
was doing in the Old Testament. The future tense clearly
shows that something new is about to be done.

The word *build* has the thought of building a house
and implies a gradual process, not an immediate act of God.
The concept of the church as a building is common in Scripture (cf. I Corinthians 3:11-15; Ephesians 2:10-22; I Peter
2:4-8).

What Christ proposes to build is described as "my
church." That which is to be constructed is the peculiar
possession of Christ as purchased by His blood and formed
by the Holy Spirit whom He sends. The use of the word
church (Gr. *ekklesia*) is the first instance of this word in
the New Testament, and in the light of subsequent revelation this seems clearly to refer to the body of Christ or the
assembly of true believers rather than to a local church
or a group of local churches or Christendom as a whole.

The vast superstructure of ecclesiasticism which characterizes the modern church can hardly be attributed to the
work of Christ. The concept that the true church is in view
here is supported by His final statement, "The gates of
hell shall not prevail against it." This implies that even
death cannot thwart the purpose of Christ in building the
church. Ultimately it will stand complete through resurrection and translation into the presence of God.

The announcement thus made by Christ, detached as it
was from His previous messages concerning the kingdom
which had been largely rejected by the Jewish people,
reflects the new divine purpose which would grow out of
His death and resurrection, namely, that which would be
formed by the Spirit of God whom Christ would send. The
exposition of His program for the church does not seem to
be found in any passage in the Synoptic Gospels. The program for the church was unfolded in principle on the last
night Christ spent with His disciples prior to His crucifixion and is contained in the Upper Room Discourse (John
13-17). Here is the great Magna Charta of the church and
the declaration of the essential principles which would
govern its character and life.

THE TEACHING OF CHRIST CONCERNING THE CHURCH AS HIS BODY

While it undoubtedly is true that the Apostle Paul was
especially chosen of God to unfold the fact of the church
as the body of Christ, it is often overlooked that a comprehensive revelation is also given by Christ Himself long before Paul was ever called to the ministry. The truth of the
church as the body of Christ is, therefore, not an exclu-
sive Pauline revelation, but was given by Christ to the
faithful eleven who gathered with Him in the Upper Room.
Delivered as it was on the night before His crucifixion, it
anticipates His rejection, resurrection, and ascension, and
deals specifically with the period between the two advents

in which God would fulfill His purpose, declared by Christ
in Matthew 16:18, to build His church.

Prominent in the revelation given by Christ to His disciples is the promise of the gift of the Holy Spirit fulfilled
on the Day of Pentecost and in the subsequent experience
of the church. Christ announced this in John 14:16, 17,
"And I will pray the Father, and he shall give you another
Comforter, that he may abide with you for ever; even the
Spirit of truth; whom the world cannot receive, because it
seeth him not, neither knoweth him: but ye know him; for
he dwelleth with you, and shall be in you." In these verses
Christ anticipated that the Spirit of God would come after
His ascension to heaven and would take up the task
of building a church or a body of true believers composed
of both Jews and Gentiles. The coming of the Spirit is in
response to the prayer of Christ and to His Father, and the
Spirit thus given is promised to abide with believers in this
present age forever, in contrast to the ministry of the Spirit
in the Old Testament in which He would come only in a
temporary way as in the case of King Saul.

The Holy Spirit is described as "the Spirit of truth"
who will be unknown and not received by the world. His
relationship to believers will be a most intimate one. Christ
contrasts what was true before and after Pentecost in the
expression, "for he dwelleth with you, and shall be in you."
Here is the theological distinction between the work of the
Spirit before Pentecost and after Pentecost. That there
was a ministry of the Spirit to saints prior to Pentecost is
evident from Scripture, but it is described as the ministry of
one who dwells *with* the saints. After Pentecost, a new relationship is described as the Holy Spirit being *in you*
(John 14:17). This is intended to represent a more intimate
identification with the Spirit and a more effective fellowship and program of divine enablement for the child of
God. The Holy Spirit thus indwelling believers was not
only to be the divine presence of God, but was to be "an-

other Comforter," that is, one who will be their constant
companion and helper.

One area in which the Holy Spirit will be especially
active is that of teaching divine truth. Christ told His
disciples in John 14:26, "But the Comforter, which is the
Holy Ghost, whom the Father will send in my name, he
shall teach you all things, and bring all things to your re-
membrance whatsoever I have said unto you." The promise
that the Holy Spirit will reveal to them the things of God is
confirmed again in John 16:12-14, "I have yet many things
to say unto you, but ye cannot bear them now. Howbeit
when he, the Spirit of truth, is come, he will guide you into
all truth: for he shall not speak of himself; but whatsoever
he shall hear, that shall he speak: and he will shew you
things to come." Though the disciples had enjoyed the
blessings of the teachings of Christ throughout His earthly
life, there were many things that they were not yet prepared to receive, including a full exposition of the purpose
of His death and resurrection and the divine purpose of
calling out Jews and Gentiles to form the body of Christ.
As Christ Himself said, "Ye cannot bear them now." He
promises, however, that the Spirit of God will guide them
and will carry to them the message which is on Christ's
heart for them. Of special emphasis in the prophecy of
Christ is the declaration that the Spirit of God would show
them "things to come," i.e., God's prophetic program. The
Spirit of God would also glorify Christ or manifest His perfection. The church was to enjoy a fullness of spiritual
revelation and intimacy in the knowledge of the Word
and will of God which far exceeds that which was experienced by saints in the Old Testament.

In addition to the promise of Christ of sending the
Spirit, He promises also to come Himself. In John 14:18
Christ said, "I will not leave you comfortless: I will come
to you." Though Christ was to be bodily in heaven, He was
to be spiritually present in the church, not simply representatively in the Holy Spirit as the Third Person, but in

His own character as the Second Person. This must not be confused with His promise of coming again in John 14:3, where it is a reference to His bodily return to receive His church. Here the spiritual presence of Christ in the church is meant, in keeping with His omnipresence. He therefore declares in John 14:18, "I will not leave you comfortless: I will come to you," which more literally translated is, "I will not leave you orphans: I am coming to you." Though they would not see Him with their physical eyes as He indicates in John 14:19, He affirms His spiritual presence with them. Later in this same chapter in verse 23, He promises that God the Father would also come and dwell with the believer. Thus the Scriptures teach that the believer is indwelt by the Triune God, God the Father, God the Son, and God the Holy Spirit, but that the primary ministry to the believer will be through the Third Person, the Holy Spirit.

In John 14:20, an additional fact is mentioned very briefly and without comment which is of great significance in view of the subsequent unfolding of the doctrine of the body of Christ. Christ not only declares that He would be with the believers, but that this would be part of the intimate relationship described simply in the words, "ye in me, and I in you." The expression, "I in you," refers to His indwelling presence, but the statement, "ye in me," affirms a new position to be given the church, the body of Christ, far more intimate and blessed in its relationship than anything ever offered to the nation Israel in the Old Testament.

The expression, "ye in me," is a specific indication that truth concerning the church as the body of Christ was revealed to His disciples even before the Day of Pentecost. Though they probably did not comprehend it at the time, it nevertheless anticipated the new relationship. Instead of being related to God as Israel was by covenant relationship and by being members of a chosen physical race, the church was to have a spiritual unity with Christ in which they would be identified with Christ, the Head of the church, would be members of His body, and would constitute together an organism with a living union rather than an association based essentially either on race or covenant. In the new relationship, racial background was to lose its significance and geographic connotation would be ignored. The important fact was their personal union with Jesus Christ and to all fellow believers. The subsequent truth of the body of Christ as enlarged in the Pauline letters gives substance to this preliminary declaration.

The Upper Room Discourse is replete with spiritual and moral truths relating to the church, including the central concept that disciples of Christ should be made known by their love for one another (John 13:34, 35). The intimacy of the new relationship is unfolded in the figure of the vine and the branches in John 15. Here the doctrine of the church as the body of Christ is given a natural illustration, Christ Himself being the vine and the individual members being the branches. The figure is designed to show living union and at the same time to illustrate the principles of bearing fruit for God in the new relationship. The disciples are instructed in John 15:7, "If ye abide in me, and my words abide in you, ye shall ask what ye will, and it shall be done unto you." It was necessary not only to have position in Christ which would be true of all believers, but it was also necessary for them to abide in that relationship, that is, to enter experientially into the dependence and yieldedness which is essential to a true member of Christ.

As they sought to bear fruit for God, they needed to have the guidance of God's revelation implied in "my word." Their program must be God's program as revealed for His church. When their program had this character, Christ told them, "Ye shall ask what ye will, and it shall be done unto you." The marvelous power of prayer depends in the present age not only upon our position in Christ, but upon our right to pray in His name, and thereby accomplish the will of God. Those who thus enter into the precious provision of God for His own are assured that they will bring forth much fruit.

In the concluding portion of the Upper Room Discourse containing the high priestly prayer of Christ (John 17), a series of petitions are recorded which constitute the major chart of the divine purpose for the present age. These include the following elements: (1) that Christ should be glorified (v. 1; cp. Philippians 2:9-11; (2) the security and safety of saints in the present age from the world (v. 11) and Satan (v. 15); (3) the sanctification of believers (v. 17); (4) that believers in the present age should be one as the Father and the Son are one (vv. 21, 22, 23); (5) that a testimony may be given before the world bringing some to faith in Christ (vv. 20, 21, 23); (6) that believers may be with Christ in glory (v. 24); (7) that the love of Christ might be in the believers (v. 26). In connection with these truths, the Lord refers to eternal life which is possessed by believers in the church (17:2, 3), and to His work of intercession for them (vv. 9, 15, 20, 24). Taken as a whole, the high-priestly prayer of Christ in John 17 is a panoramic view of God's divine purpose in this present age, and is in sharp distinction to His purpose for Israel in many respects, since it is a revelation of God's divine purpose for the church composed of both Jews and Gentiles.

THE FORMATION OF THE CHURCH AT PENTECOST

The Day of Pentecost records the coming of the Spirit to the world in obvious parallelism to the coming of Christ as a babe to Bethlehem. Instead of being incarnate in human flesh, the Holy Spirit was to be clothed with the church which is Christ's body.

The Day of Pentecost is anticipated not only in the pronouncement of Christ in the Upper Room relative to the coming of the Spirit, but in the specific promise given on the day of ascension as recorded in Acts 1:5, "For John truly baptized with water; but ye shall be baptized with the Holy Ghost not many days hence." He further promises in Acts 1:8: "But ye shall receive power, after that the Holy Ghost is come upon you: and ye shall be witnesses unto me both in Jerusalem, and in all Judea, and in Samaria, and unto the uttermost part of the earth."

In keeping with these promises, in the second chapter of Acts as the disciples were gathered in a public meeting on the Day of Pentecost the experience of the coming of the ·Spirit was realized by the church. It was accompanied with the outer phenomena of "a sound from heaven as of a rushing mighty wind" and the appearance of "cloven tongues like as of fire" which appeared on each one of them. The immediate result was, "They were all filled with the Holy Ghost, and began to speak with other tongues as the Spirit gave them utterance" (Acts 2:4). As the multitude gathered when the report reached them of these unusual happenings, they heard Peter's sermon which ended in pub'ic confession of faith on the part of three thousand who were baptized in public demonstration of their faith in Christ.

The significance of the Day of Pentecost is clearly one of a new milestone in the undertaking of God. It set apart the period prior to Pentecost as belonging to the old order and signified that the period following Pentecost would be a fulfillment of a dispensation in which the Holy Spirit would have prominence. The subsequent theological interpretation of the Day of Pentecost is found first in Peter's experience in Acts 10 and 11 and in Paul's declaration concerning the baptism of the Spirit in I Corinthians 12:13.

In Peter's experience, he was instructed to partake of unclean things by his vision from heaven (Acts 10:9-16). Peter was commanded by the Spirit of God to accompany the Gentiles who came for him to bring him to Cornelius the centurion (Acts 10:17-20). When Peter preached his sermon as recorded in Acts 10:34-43 relating that Jesus Christ was indeed the Saviour through His death and resurrection and that remission of sins is promised those who believe in Him, there was the immediate response of faith on the part of his hearers. The Scriptures record the astonishment of Peter as he sees poured out upon these Gentiles the same gift of the Holy Spirit which had characterized the church on the Day of Pentecost.

In the subsequent explanation of Peter to those who had criticized him for eating with Gentiles, he explained in Acts 11:15-17: "And as I began to speak, the Holy Ghost fell on them, as on us at the beginning. Then remembered I the Word of the Lord, how that he said, John indeed baptized with water; but ye shall be baptized with the Holy Ghost. Forasmuch then as God gave them the like gift as he did unto us, who believed on the Lord Jesus Christ; what was I, that I could withstand God?"

. In his explanation, the Apostle Peter clearly identified the experience of Cornelius and his friends as being the same as that which occurred on the Day of Pentecost, namely, that they had been baptized with the Holy Ghost. He also referred to the Day of Pentecost as "the beginning." This is a plain indication that something new began on the Day of Pentecost, namely, the body of Christ formed by the baptism of the Spirit.

In I Corinthians 12:13 in connection with the discussion of the church as the body of Christ, the Apostle Paul declared: "For by one Spirit are we all baptized into one body, whether we be Jews or Gentiles, whether we be bond or free; and have been all made to drink into one Spirit." Here is revealed that the baptism of the Spirit is the universal work of the Spirit which places every true believer in Christ into the body of Christ, the church. This is accomplished for them regardless of whether they are Jews or Gentiles, whether they are bond or free, and is the basis by which they participate in all the ministries of the Spirit described as drinking into one Spirit in this text. In contrast to the filling of the Spirit which is experienced only by some Christians, the baptism of the Spirit forming the body of Christ is the structural work of the Spirit by which the body is formed and properly related to Christ, its Head.

The Day of Pentecost, therefore, is the fulfillment of the original pronouncement of Christ in Matthew 16:18.

THE PAULINE DOCTRINE OF THE ONE BODY

At least seven figures are used in the New Testament to describe the relationship between Christ and the church: (1) Christ as the Shepherd and the church as the sheep (John 10:1-16); (2) the vine and the branches (John 15:1-11); (3) the last Adam and the new creation (I Corinthians 15:45; II Corinthians 5:17); (4) Christ as the head and the church as the body (Ephesians 1:20-23; 3:6; 4:11-16); (5) Christ as the foundation and the church as the building (Ephesians 2:19-22; I Corinthians 3:11-15); (6) Christ as the high priest and the church as a royal priesthood (I Peter 2:9; Revelation 1:6; cp. Hebrews 8:1-6); (7) Christ as the bridegroom and the church as the bride (Matthew 22:2; 25:1-13; II Corinthians 11:2; Revelation 19:7-9).

Each of the seven figures relating Christ to the church has its own body of truth, but central in the theological concept of the church is the revelation concerning the church as the one body. This truth is introduced in Ephesians 1: 20-22 where it is related to the resurrected Christ and His exaltation in glory resulting in all authority being put under Him, including the church, His body. As expressed by Paul, the power of God "hath put all things under his feet, and gave him to be head over all things to the church, which is his body, the fulness of him that filleth all in all." The true church composed of all true believers is here described under the symbolism of the human body being subject to its head and accordingly united to the head in a living union.

In the second chapter of Ephesians, this truth is expanded in the declaration that the church is a new creation "created in Christ Jesus unto good works" (Ephesians 2:10). In the discussion which follows, Paul contrasts the situation of the Ephesian Christians in the past, before their

salvation, as being uncircumcised Gentiles, and states, "that
at that time ye were without Christ, being aliens from the
commonwealth of Israel, and strangers from the covenants
of promise, having no hope, and without God in the world."
The desperate spiritual state of all Gentiles is thus graphically described and forms a stark background for their
new position in Christ.

Beginning in Ephesians 2:13, Paul lists the tremendous
factors which have been changed now that they are Christians: "But now in Christ Jesus ye who were sometimes far
off are made nigh by the blood of Christ."

Having been redeemed, he states that Christ "is our
peace, who hath made both one, and hath broken down the
middle wall of partition between us" (Ephesians 2:14).
The reference is to the contrast between Jew and Gentile
which in Christ is eliminated in that both have been made
one in the body of Christ. This is enforced by the verses
which follow in which the apostle states that the enmity
which separated Jew and Gentile is now abolished and in
grace Christ has made "in himself of twain one new man,
so making peace" (Ephesians 2:15). The new man is another reference to the unity of the body of Christ. This
is made plain in the verse in Ephesians 2:16 which follows,
"And that he might reconcile both unto God in one body
by the cross, having slain the enmity thereby." The figure
of the one body is supported by the concept of the church
as the household of God built upon Christ the chief corner-
stone and fitted together as a holy temple unto the Lord
constituting a habitation of the Spirit (Ephesians 2:19-22).

With this general introduction to the subject of the
church as the body of Christ, the apostle unfolds its character as a mystery in the third chapter of Ephesians. Paul
reveals that the doctrine of the church as the body of Christ
was a subject of special revelation to him (Ephesians
3:1-3). He states further that the truth of the church as
the body of Christ, "in other ages was not made unto the
sons of men, as it is now revealed unto his holy apostles

and prophets by the Spirit; that the Gentiles should be fellowheirs, and of the same body, and partakers of his promise in Christ by the gospel." In an effort to evade what seems to be the plain teaching of this passage of Scripture that the church is something new and the subject of new revelation, these verses have been interpreted by some as merely indicating additional truth rather than a new revelation. Seizing upon the word *as*, the thought is advanced that the truth concerning the church was revealed in the Old Testament but not in the same way as it is revealed now.

The uniform use of the word *mystery* in the New Testament, however, is that it refers to truth which was "not made known unto the sons of men" in the Old Testament. A normative instance is found in Colossians 1:26 where the statement is made, "Even the mystery which hath been hid from ages and generations, but now is made manifest to his saints." In Ephesians 3:5, the same meaning is intended. The contrast is not between degrees of revelation, but between that which was not revealed in the Old Testament but is now revealed unto the apostles and prophets of the New Testament. That this absolute character of contrast between what is hidden and what is revealed is intended is brought out plainly in verse 6 where the contents of the mystery is said to be the revelation "that the Gentiles shall be fellowheirs, and of the same body, and partakers of his promise in Christ by the gospel." In the Old Testament, Gentiles and Jews are distinguished beginning in Genesis 12 and continuing until the Day of Pentecost. Jews and Gentiles are never equated in the Old Testament, as the Jews are the chosen people in contrast to the Gentiles who are outside the covenant. This is brought out even in the context of Ephesians as, for instance, in 2:12 where the lot of the Jew and the Gentile is sharply contrasted.

The idea that Gentiles should be on exactly the same plane as Israelites and, furthermore, in the intimate relationship as being members of the same body, is absolutely foreign to the Old Testament. According to Isaiah 61:5, 6, the Gentiles are pictured as being the servants and Israel as the priests of God. While it is true that the Gentiles were promised blessings in the future millennial kingdom, they are never given equality with the Jews in the Old Testament. What was new and unpredicted as far as the Old Testament is concerned, here forms the content of the special revelation given Paul concerning the church, the body of Christ. A Jew or a Gentile who through faith in Christ becomes a member of the body of Christ, by so much is detached from his former situation, and his prophetic program then becomes that of the church rather than that of Jews or Gentiles as such. It is only as the prophetic program of the church as the body of Christ is distinguished from that of Israel or that of the Gentiles that confusion can be avoided in the interpretation of unfulfilled prophecy.

The subject of the church as the one body is given further revelation in Ephesians 4 where it is declared that in keeping with the figure of a body, each individual member in the church has his particular gift, and "the whole body fitly joined together and compacted by that which every joint supplieth, according to the effectual working in the measure of every part, maketh increase of the body unto edifying of itself in love" (Ephesians 4:16). The same truth is unfolded in Romans 12:3-8 where individuals are likened to the members of the body having different gifts and different capacities, but all essential to the perfection of the body.

Taken as a whole, the doctrine of the body of Christ is a marvelous vehicle for divine revelation, demonstrating the supreme benefits given to believers in this present age under God's divine program of grace, disregarding racial and cultural backgrounds such as are prominent in the Old Testament. In the church, all believers are on an equal plane. Though distinguished by their spiritual gifts sovereignly bestowed, they have a common destiny and program in God's unfolding of His will for the church. Central in this purpose is that declared in Ephesians 2:7, "That in the ages to come he might shew the exceeding riches of his grace and his kindness toward us through Christ Jesus." Though the grace of God is manifested in all dispensations from the salvation of Adam and Eve to the last soul that is added, the church is selected to be the supreme revelation of that grace and will constitute a display of the grace of God not only in time but in eternity to come. In a similar way, Israel was selected of God to demonstrate His faithfulness and His righteousness and through eternity will display supremely these blessed aspects.

The contrast of the church as the body of Christ to the professing church or Christendom as a whole is essential to a proper understanding of God's prophetic program. While the church as the body of Christ will have its climax in the translation of the church and its rapture into heaven with subsequent events that pertain only to those who are saved, Christendom as a whole as an ecclesiastical organization will move on into the tribulation time and fulfill the prophecies that relate to it as it ends in complete apostasy. This dual development is paralleled to some extent by prophecy relating to the godly remnant of Israel throughout history as contrasted to the nation as a whole, but the church never becomes Israel, and Israel never becomes the church.

Chapter IV

THE CHURCH IN THE END OF THE AGE

Are There Signs of the Rapture of the Church?

One of the neglected areas of prophetic study is that pertaining to the end of the church age. The assertion is often confidently made that there are no signs of the rapture of the church, as it is presented everywhere in Scripture as an imminent event. Therefore, it is argued, we should be looking for the coming of the Lord, rather than for signs that precede, as the rapture of the church is before the time of tribulation predicted in Scripture.

Most of the prophetic word relating to the end time has to do with the second coming of Christ to establish His kingdom in the earth. Prophecy is devoted to the events which precede the second coming rather than a series of events preceding the rapture itself. In the Gospel of Matthew, for instance, the general and specific signs leading up to the second coming of Christ are clearly outlined and the great tribulation is presented as the great, unmistakable sign of the second coming of Christ to the earth. In a similar way in the book of Revelation, an extended revelation is given beginning in chapter 6 of the events which will mark the end of the age preceding Christ's return to the earth. If these events follow rather than precede the rapture of the church, they cannot be taken as signs of the rapture itself.

There are, however, two bona fide areas of study relating to anticipation of the rapture itself. One of these has to do with preparation for events which will follow the rapture. There are extensive preparations in the present world scene which seem to be a foreshadowing and preparation for events which will follow the rapture. If so, these would constitute evidence that the rapture itself may be near. These signs will be presented in a later discussion. Another important area, however, is the Scriptural description of the church at the end of the age. According to Scripture, there will be a progression of fulfilled prophecy in the church age itself which will be observable before the rapture even though its final form will not come into existence until after the true church has been caught up to be with the Lord. In a word, the Scriptures predict that there will be a growing apostasy or departure from the Lord as the church age progresses, and its increase can be understood as a general indication that the rapture itself is near. The Scriptures dealing with this subject are those which describe the church in the end of the age. These are in contrast to events of the tribulation itself which come to pass subsequent to the rapture.

THE HISTORY OF APOSTASY

The concept of apostasy or departure from the faith is by no means a new idea, but can be traced throughout Scripture beginning in the Garden of Eden. There the taunting question expressed by the serpent to the woman, "Yea, hath God said?" (Genesis 3:1), introduced unbelief to the human race which has borne its sad fruit through the centuries since Adam. Basically, apostasy has always been a departure from faith in God's revealed Word, whether oral or written. It was that unbelief which inspired the first sin and in subsequent generations made necessary the terrible judgments of God upon human sin. In the Old Testament, it took the form of questioning God's revelation concerning sacrifices as revealed in Cain's rejection of blood sacrifices as a way of approach to God which ended in the murder of his brother, Abel. It was this same attitude of unbelief which rejected the preaching of righteousness through Noah even as he was building the ark which ended in the terrible judgment of the flood. It was the departure from the revealed worship and will of God which led to the construction of the Tower of Babel and the introduction of God's plan for Abram and his seed. It was lack of apprehension of the plan of God for Abram's posterity that caused Jacob to leave the land and ultimately to find his way down into Egypt to escape the famine. It was through unbelief that Israel failed to conquer the land under Joshua and to ignore in subsequent generations the solemn warning of Moses. It was unbelief that produced the awful immorality of the period of the Judges. It was unbelief that led Israel into idolatry which ended in the captivities of Assyria and Babylon. Finally, it was unbelief which blinded the eyes of Israel in rejecting the credentials of their Messiah and Saviour.

The history of the church subsequent to the close of the canon is also a sad record of departure from God. The church, kept pure through persecution in the early centuries, soon began to depart from the faith contained in the Scriptures once the church became a popular organization under Constantine. The first casualty was a departure from chiliasm, or the doctrine of the premillennial coming of Christ and the establishment of His millennial kingdom. Though the early church as well as the church of the Middle Ages seems to have clung resolutely to the idea of a bodily second coming as indicated by their creeds, the precious truths of the imminent coming of the Lord for His church and the establishment of Christ's righteous reign on earth soon lost its prominence. The teaching arose that Christ could not come back until a thousand years after the time of the apostles. This was based on the erroneous idea that the church was already in the millennium and that the millennium had to run its course before Christ could return.

The next important casualty in Scriptural doctrine was the departure from grace beginning with Augustine and his theology. While holding resolutely to the doctrine of human depravity with its corresponding need of divine grace,

Augustine and subsequent theologians in the Roman Catholic Church maintained that grace was channeled through the church and the sacraments and, apart from this medium, there could be no true salvation or bestowal of grace. As a result, the great doctrine of justification by faith, the truth of the fullness and power of the Holy Spirit, and the truth that believers had immediate access to the throne of grace without an earthly priest as mediator became dim. Soon the authority of the Scriptures as the Word of God became subordinate to the authority of the church, and the interpretation of the church took precedence over the teaching ministry and illumination of the Holy Spirit. The Word of God, thus shackled and to a large extent kept from the people, cast its restricted light on the darkness of the Middle Ages.

The Protestant Reformation, of course, brought a fresh study of great essentials of Christian truth. Once again the Word of God was made its own authority. The great doctrine of justification by faith was proclaimed. The Roman priesthood was thrust aside in favor of the clear teaching that every Christian is a priest once he has put his faith in Christ and can have immediate access to the throne of God in the name of his Saviour. Likewise the grace of God came as an immediate bestowal of the Holy Spirit. Though Protestantism did not completely shake loose the sacramental idea of the Romanish system, it was a new state of freedom. Every man now could interpret the Bible guided by the Holy Spirit as his teacher and could revel in the abundance of God's sanctifying truth.

The Protestant Reformation, however, had barely begun before the sad evidence of further departure began. In the centuries that followed, the enlightenment freed men's minds and wills to believe and do as they pleased. No longer shackled by the dogma of the church, men could achieve new understanding of the physical and philosophic realm. Soon higher criticism began to rear its ugly head, and rationalism demanded that Christian doctrines be submitted to the bar of reason. Mystics arose who made experience the criteria of theological judgment. Critics began to divide the Bible and challenge traditional views of authorship and historical backgrounds. Apostasy invaded Protestantism with the same devastating effect it had had on the Roman Church.

The departure from the doctrine of infallible inspiration of the original writings in the nineteenth century in Europe soon found its way to the Western Hemisphere and precipitated the modernist-fundamentalist controversies of the first quarter of the twentieth century. With the departure from the doctrine of inspiration, there came ultimately a like departure from the doctrine of Christ. The virgin birth began to be questioned and declared unimportant. The deity of Christ was reduced to a divine quality rather than to a state of divine being. The bodily resurrection of Christ was made a spiritual resurrection instead of a literal raising of His body from the grave. Open skepticism arose within the church concerning doctrines of final judgment and of heaven and hell. The love of God was regarded as making impossible a God of righteous judgment.

The twentieth century marked not only the departure from Biblical Christianity to an extent never before witnessed in the history of the church, but also signaled the rise of new and confusing heresies. Multiplied cults and new forms of religion arose with varied degrees of allegiance to Christianity, a new combination of old errors came into being, of which the most powerful and important is neo-orthodoxy. The growth and character of apostasy in the world today, when viewed in the light of predictions in the Scripture concerning the last days of the church, seem to be a clear parallel to what one might have a right to expect in the days immediately preceding the rapture.

THE GENERAL CHARACTER OF HERESY
IN THE LAST DAYS

One of the major revelations concerning apostasy in the last days is that contained in I Timothy 4:1-3: "Now the

Spirit speaketh expressly, that in the latter times some shall depart from the faith, giving heed to seducing spirits, and doctrines of devils; speaking lies in hypocrisy; having their conscience seared with a hot iron; forbidding to marry, and commanding to abstain from meats, which God hath created to be received with thanksgiving of them which believe and know the truth."

This revelation given by Paul to Timothy according to the passage itself has to do with the "latter times." The character of departure from the faith is specified as containing the following items: (1) giving heed to seducing spirits, and doctrines of devils; (2) speaking lies in hypocrisy; (3) having a conscience which is insensible; (4) forbidding to marry; (5) and commanding to abstain from certain food. While these factors can be seen to some extent throughout the history of the church, they are increasingly evident in modern Christianity. The satanic character of departure from the faith is evident in the confusion existing in the church regarding its proper theology. That which is contrary to the Scriptures is offered as the truth of God. Much that is traveling in the guise of religion is to spiritually minded Christians nothing other than an evidence of the power of Satan with all its deceptiveness. False doctrines are advanced without any attempt to relate them to the Word of God. In the name of religion much is promoted that demonstrates an insensitivity to the morality and holiness commanded of true Christians.

Of special interest is the prophecy that in the end of the age there will be prohibition of marriage and requirement to abstain from certain foods. It is evident in the Roman Church today that priests are forbidden to marry on the ground that the single estate is more holy than the married estate, something which is not taught in the Word of God. It should be clear to any reader of Scripture that the creation of Eve was God's plan, not Adam's, and that the command to populate the earth by bearing children preceded rather than followed the fall. Though in individual

cases it may not be God's will for some to marry, as illustrated in the case of Paul, others were in the will of God
in the married estate as in the case of the Apostle Peter.
The prohibition regarding marriage originates in the com-
mands of men, not in the Word of God, and is a sign of the
encroaching false religion which characterizes the end of
the age in contrast to the true faith contained in the Scriptures.

Another obvious factor is the religious custom to abstain from meats on Friday and to refrain from certain foods
during Lent. This again is a man-made invention and certainly not taught in the Word of God. As the apostle indicates, if the food is that which God has created to be
received with thanksgiving, then it can be eaten without
violation of the moral will of God. The encroaching ritual-
ism represented in these two items of I Timothy 4:3 is
typical of religion as it attempts to curtail freedom which
belongs to the child of God under grace. The fact that
these three verses provide such an accurate picture of the
contemporary scene leads to the conclusion that that which
Paul described as coming to pass in the latter time is already
being fulfilled in the professing church today.

THE DENIAL OF THE PERSON AND WORK OF CHRIST

One of the major sections on apostasy in the last days
is that provided in II Peter 2-3. In these two chapters a
comprehensive picture of the false teachers of the last days
is given. In II Peter 2:1, 2, the major features of apostasy
are predicted: "But there were false prophets also among
the people, even as there shall be false teachers among you,
who privily shall bring in damnable heresies, even denying the Lord that bought them, and bring upon themselves
swift destruction. And many shall follow their pernicious
ways; by reason of whom the way of truth shall be evil
spoken of."

According to Peter, there would arise in the church
period false teachers corresponding to the false prophets

which Israel endured. These false teachers would by stealth bring in that which he described as "damnable heresies" or "destructive heresies." It is clear here that the apostle is not dealing with minor variations within the Christian faith such as often characterized difference of opinion within the orthodox church. It is rather that he predicts departures of such character that they are destructive completely to the Christian faith, that is, make impossible the salvation of those who adhere to them. He states that these heresies can be described as "denying the Lord that bought them" with the result that they will bring upon themselves swift destruction.

It would be almost impossible to state more succinctly the fundamental denial of the Christian faith which characterizes our day, for modern Christianity has indeed denied the Lord that bought them. This is actually a twofold error which is having a devastating effect upon the church. It is, first of all, the denial of the person of Christ and, second, a denial of His work.

It is characteristic of modern liberalism to teach that Jesus Christ was not born of a virgin, but actually was the natural child of Joseph and Mary. In attempting to explain the unusual influence of Christ upon His generation, and to account for the formation of the Christian church, it is often admitted that Christ was an unusual person even if He were only an ordinary man.

Modern liberals often explain that Jesus as a lad was an unusual person. He had an unusual consciousness of God and an unusual devotion to the will of God. Liberals explain that this was so noticeable in His character that people began to identify Him with God and called Him the Son of God. Accordingly, they point to Christ as the great example. They say that just as Christ became the Son of God by yielding to the will of God, by thinking God's thoughts, by worshiping God, and by doing God's will so others also can follow in His example and also become the sons of God.

From the standpoint of orthodox Christianity, of course, this is indeed a damnable heresy. It is affirming that Christ was an ordinary man who became divine in His experience but not in His person. It by-passes the whole matter of Christ's substitutionary atonement, the natural depravity of men, and the need for supernatural grace. Though often taught cleverly and covered up with evangelical terminology, it is all the more a deceptive device to take people from the truth as it is in Christ Jesus.

Modern neo-orthodoxy, while not straying as far as many liberals have gone, nevertheless tends to ignore the question whether Christ existed from all eternity past as the Second Person. They tend to by-pass the problem of whether there was indeed a genuine incarnation of the infinite God and man and whether Christ as a man was indeed all that He was before as the infinite God. Though the expression "Son of God" and the adjective "divine" are often attributed to Christ, it is not at all clear whether they mean by this something distinctive and unique. There is far more denial of the person of Christ in modern Christianity than is immediately apparent. It is probable that never before in the history of the church has there been more subversion of the true doctrine of Christology than there is in the contemporary theology of the church.

If denial of the person of Christ is common, even more so is there denial of the concept that Christ bought us. The idea that Christ is a substitute for sinners, that He died as a Lamb upon the cross, that He bore our sins as the Scriptures indicate, and by the shedding of His blood effected a judicial basis for our salvation, is all most offensive to the modern mind. To modern men the death of Christ is at best a noble example of sincerity of purpose or a demonstration of the wickedness of man, in that man would crucify such a noble character. To the liberal, the love of God is redemptive itself apart from the sacrifice of Christ and in effect liberals do exactly what Peter predicts, they deny that the Lord bought us with His shed blood. While there may be differences of opinion on the interpretation of prophecy within the body of Christ, which do not affect the eternal salvation of those who hold these opinions, it should be obvious to every careful student of the Word of God that a denial of the person of Christ and a denial of the sacrifice of Christ strikes a blow at indispensable Christian truths and, as Peter predicts, those who deny this will bring upon themselves the righteous judgment of God.

Peter goes on to prophesy that many will follow their pernicious ways. It is sadly true that the way of truth is in a minority in the modern day. While churches beautiful in architecture and rich in appointment are evident in every city, their existence and their popularity is not in itself an evidence that the truth is being preached. Instead, Bible-believing Christians are sometimes viewed as cultic, as abnormal, as reactionary, as anti-intellectual, and as those who do not keep abreast of the times. Not many churches today welcome either to the pulpit or to the pew those who expound apostolic doctrine which is normally considered orthodox in the history of the church. Instead, those who have platitudes of good works, who preach interesting but unchallenging sermons and who leave their congregation undisturbed seem to be in the ascendancy.

The Apostle Peter spares no words in describing these false teachers. He accused them of "covetousness," of "feigned words," of making "merchandise of you," as being subject to God's "judgment," and "damnation" (II Peter 2:3). He accuses them of walking "after the flesh in the lust of uncleanness," of being such as "despise government," who are "presumptuous," "self-willed," who "speak evil of dignities" (II Peter 2:10). He declares that they are "as natural brute beasts, made to be taken and destroyed," who "speak evil of things that they understand not" and who "shall utterly perish in their own corruption" (II Peter 2:12). He declares that they "shall receive the reward of unrighteousness, as they that count it pleasure to riot in

the daytime" (II Peter 2:13). Even in the observance
of the Lord's Supper, they are "spots" and "blemishes" (II
Peter 2:13). Their immorality is revealed in that they have
"eyes full of adultery," and "cannot cease from sin; be-
guiling unstable souls" (II Peter 2:14). They are "covetous,"
"cursed children"; "they have forsaken the right way, and
are gone astray, following the way of Balaam the son of
Bosor, who loved the wages of unrighteousness" (II Peter
2:14, 15). They "are wells without water, clouds that are
carried with a tempest; to whom the mist of darkness is re-
served for ever" (II Peter 2:17). They "speak great swell-
ing words of vanity, they allure through the lusts of the
flesh" (II Peter 2:18). They promise "liberty" though
"they themselves are the servants of corruption" (II Peter
2:19). They are said to fulfill "the true proverb, The dog
is turned to his own vomit again; and the sow that was
washed to her wallowing in the mire" (II Peter 2:22).

In the Epistle of Jude, a similar indictment is leveled
against those who are apostates. They are said to be "ungodly men, turning the grace of our God into lascivious-
ness, and denying the only Lord God, and our Lord Jesus
Christ" (v. 4). Jude does not spare denunciation of apostate
teachers, comparing them to the apostates in Sodom and
Gomorrah, both in their rebellion against God and against
Christian moral standards. In most details, Jude parallels
II Peter.

From these extended references to the moral character of apostasy, it is clear that God takes a far more serious view both of the theology and morality of false religion
than is common among Christians today. The Word of God
strips the apostates of any veneer of respectability, sincerity
of motives, or worthy purpose, and reveals them for what
they are, tools of Satan and the enemies of Christ and of
all who love Him.

This shocking portrayal of the character of false teachers and their doctrines is too little realized by the church of
Jesus Christ today. Misguided by religious phrases and the
pomp and ceremony of modern Christianity, with its ap-

pearance of scholarship and its supposed progress in theology, many today are not willing to face the stark reality of heresy within the church and the widespread departure from Biblical faith. Here in the words of Peter and forming this portion of the inspired Word of God, heresy is unmasked and the contemporary church is seen from God's viewpoint. The hypocrisy, immorality, vanity, and emptiness of modern liberalism has its culmination in denying the Lord who died for a lost humanity.

DENIAL OF THE SECOND COMING OF CHRIST

In the form of a postscript to the Apostle Peter's general description of apostates in the last days, the prediction is added that there would also be departure from the truth of the second coming of Christ. Peter writes: "Knowing this first, that there shall come in the last days scoffers, walking after their own lusts, and saying, Where is the promise of his coming: for since the fathers fell asleep, all things continue as they were from the beginning of the creation" (II Peter 3:3, 4). In this passage false teachers are described as "scoffers, walking after their own lusts." On the one hand they are unbelievers, that is, those who will not accept the Word of God concerning the coming of the Lord, and, second, they are motivated by their own lusts and immorality.

It is an obvious fact that modern liberals scoff at the second coming of Christ, motivated primarily by their desire to avoid the doctrine of divine judgment upon sin which is commonly associated with it in Scripture. The widespread denial of a bodily return of Christ is prompted by a desire to avoid the teaching of Scripture concerning the revelation of righteousness which will accompany fulfillment of prophecy relating to the second coming. These false teachers approach the doctrine of the second coming with a question born of unbelief as they ask, "Where is the promise of his second coming?" They attempt to support their unbelief by the statement, "Since the fathers fell asleep, all things continue as they were from the beginning of the creation."

Both the questions raised and the supporting evidence is, of course, contradicted by the facts of history. There is no logical support of the idea that a delay in the second coming of Christ is a valid argument against its ultimate fulfillment. Many prophecies in the Scriptures were fulfilled thousands of years after their deliverance, and there is no reason to believe that the passage of time alters the sure Word of God. The argument that all things have continued undisturbed since creation is contradicted by many Scriptures.

Peter points out that their assumption that all things have continued without interruption from beginning of creation is an absolute untruth. The entire Word of God bears its testimony to the fact that God does intervene in human events, that He does guide human history, that both naturally and supernaturally the providential government of God is manifest in the history of the world. An illustration is afforded first of all in the doctrine of creation itself in that God by His own command caused the earth to stand out of the water and in the water and created the starry heavens above. In verse 6 he refers to the earth as being destroyed by being overflowed with water. This is usually considered a reference to the flood of Noah. Peter says that just as God once destroyed the earth with water, so it is predicted He will in the future destroy the earth by fire.

Though not mentioned by Peter, it is obvious that the history of Scripture contains many other interventions of God into the natural situation. Many of His chastisements of Israel are illustrations of the fact that all things have not continued as they were from the beginning of creation. The greatest intervention of all was in the first coming of Christ when God invaded the human sphere in the form of the incarnation. The literal fulfillment of promises pertaining to the first coming is a foreshadowing of the literal fulfillment of promises pertaining to the second coming. For liberals, of course, who deny a genuine incarnation and who do not accept the testimony of Scripture, probably the appeal to nature used by Peter is the most valid and telling argument.

The promise of a future destruction by fire is joined to an explanation as to why the second coming has not already been fulfilled. As Peter explains it, in the first place, "one day is with the Lord as a thousand years, and a thousand years as one day" (II Peter 3:8). By this he means that time is not a factor with God in the same sense as it is with man, in that a thousand years pass as quickly for God as one day does with man. On the other hand, he means that there is the same planning in one day of human experience as there is in a thousand years of human history. God views the world in its history both from the microscopic and telescopic viewpoint. For this reason, the passage of several thousand years since the first coming of Christ is no argument at all that the second coming will not be fulfilled in God's time.

In contemporary theology, however, even liberals have been forced to give renewed attention to the doctrine of the second coming. Liberals have been jarred from their complacency by the events of the first half of the twentieth century including World War II. They have had to face the fact that the world could come to a sudden and dramatic end and that such an end is not beyond reason and certainly not beyond the Scriptural revelation. As the second half of the twentieth century began, however, it soon became clear that this renewed attention to the doctrine of the second coming of Christ was not a return to the Biblical truth, but rather an attempt to evade its plain teaching. The second coming of Christ is thus regarded as a spiritual experience, as a divine intervention into human consciousness or possibly as fulfilled in the death of the believer. The dramatic events related in Scripture as preceding and following the second coming of Christ are usually ignored.

Further light is given on the real cause for delay in Christ's return to the earth in II Peter 3:9: "The Lord is not slack concerning his promise, as some men count slackness; but is longsuffering to us-ward, not willing that any should perish, but that all should come to repentance." The reason for the seeming delay in the coming of the Lord is not due to slackness or inability to fulfill His promise, but is inspired instead by the longsuffering of God who wishes to extend mercy to the ultimate limit, permitting all who will come and escape the divine judgment which attends the second coming. God is "not willing that any should perish, but that all should come to repentance." This is His desire and though the Scriptures clearly reveal that God's heart will not be completely satisfied in this respect in that many will perish, it is the will of God that opportunity should be afforded as long as possible.

In due time, however, the Day of the Lord will come. Peter describes this in verse 10 as a time "in which the heavens shall pass away with a great noise, and the elements shall melt with fervent heat, the earth also and the works that are therein shall be burned up" (II Peter 3:10). From Revelation 20:11; 21:1, we learn that this will take place at the end of the Day of the Lord rather than at its beginning, that is, the Day of the Lord is viewed as the extended period of time between the rapture of the church and the end of the millennium, and will be climaxed by destruction of the present heaven and earth and the creation of a new heaven and earth.

It is stated plainly that the earth and the works in it are going to be burned up. According to II Peter 3:11: "All these things shall be dissolved." This could not be at the beginning of the millennium, for life continues including identifiable geographic locations such as the Mount of Olives, the city of Jerusalem, and the nations which surround Israel. Peter states clearly that God's ultimate purpose is something more than simply Christ coming back to earth. It is the fulfillment of God's plan to bring in the eternal state where righteousness will reign and where the saints will enjoy the blessings of the grace of God throughout eternity. Those who scoff at the second coming of Christ are thereby denying the total of God's program prophetically for the world and will participate in what Peter refers to in II Peter 3:7 as "the day of judgment and perdition of ungodly men."

The prediction that there will be scoffing concerning the second coming of Christ is sadly fulfilled in the twentieth century. Few pulpits today proclaim a bodily second coming of Christ to the earth. In the minds of many professing Christians, truths concerning the second coming are considered as proper items of faith only for cults and those outside the main body of Christendom. Countless thousands of professing Christians are totally ignorant concerning the facts of Scripture which describe the second coming of Christ.

Though modern liberals have written in recent days numerous works dealing with the second coming of Christ, an examination of their contributions revealed that they are not talking about the second coming of Christ as presented in the Bible, but are using the terminology to refer to crisis in Christian experience or to the death of the believer. Actually, though using the terminology, they do not believe in a bodily second coming of Christ and thereby contribute to the confusion and unbelief that is characteristic of modern Christendom in relation to these great truths. Never before in the history of the church has the truth of the second coming of Christ been so vaguely held so far as the church at large is concerned as in our day. Actually the modern church denies the very idea of the prophetic and declares that it is impossible for anyone to predict the future whether it be the second coming of Christ or any other event in prophecy. Thus, unbelief is on the throne and faith and hope are shoved aside.

COLDNESS AND INDIFFERENCE IN THE CHURCH

In the letter to the church at Laodicea, the last of the seven churches of Asia, the charge was made that they were lukewarm: "I know thy works, that thou art neither cold nor hot: I would thou wert cold or hot. So then be cause thou art lukewarm, and neither cold nor hot, I will spue thee out of my mouth" (Revelation 3:15, 16). Whether or not the seven churches of Asia are prophetic of the entire age as many have held, the charge against the church at Laodicea is remarkably accurate for the church today. In contrast to the church of the Middle Ages which was dead, the modern church fulfills the description of being neither hot nor cold, quite self-content with its supposed riches and attainment. It is characteristic of much of the modern church to say complimentary words about Christ, but to avoid any. clear testimony concerning His unique deity and His eternity. There is constant reference to "Jesus of Nazareth" but less clear is the question as to whether He was what He claimed to be, one with the Father in being as well as in fellowship.

The church today is too evidently overtaken by its worldliness. The lives of its people are often indistinguishable from those outside the church. Its prayer meetings are the poorest attended meetings of the week. Its congregations build great cathedrals to house their own worship, but often have little concern for the dying millions who have never heard of Christ. In some of our major denominations, it takes over forty congregations to support one full-time missionary on a foreign field. Rejection of such a pseudo-Christianity is evident in the striking statement, "I will spue thee out of my mouth" (Revelation 3:16). If the Laodicean church is characteristic of the church of the last days, it does not foreshadow any glorious triumph such as is prophesied in postmillennialism.

In II Timothy 3:1-5, there is a graphic picture of apostasy in the last days. Paul described it as a time of peril (II Timothy 3:1), a time when "men shall be lovers of their own selves, covetous, boasters, proud, blasphemers, disobedient to parents, unthankful, unholy, without natural affection, trucebreakers, false accusers, incontinent, fierce, despisers of those that are good, traitors, heady, highminded, lovers of pleasures more than lovers of God; having a form of godliness, but denying the power thereof: from such turn away" (II Timothy 3:2-5). His summary of the situation at the end time in II Timothy 3:13 makes it clear that the end of the age will be one of apostasy, "But evil men and seducers shall wax worse and worse, deceiving, and being deceived."

The increment of evil, the growth of hypocrisy, selfishness, and unbelief within the bounds of professing Christendom are according to Scriptures the signs of the approaching end of the age. Though there are thousands of faithful congregations and many pious souls still bearing a faithful testimony to Christ in our modern day, it is hardly true that the majority of Christendom is bearing a true testimony. It is the exception rather than the rule for the great fundamentals of the church to ring from the pulpit and for the pew to manifest the transforming grace of God in life and sacrificial devotion. In a word, the last days of the church on earth are days of apostasy, theologically and morally, days of unbelief, and days that will culminate in divine judgment.

THE RELATION OF THE RAPTURE TO THE APOSTASY

In the church at Thessalonica, a misunderstanding concerning prophecy is corrected in II Thessalonians 2. Apparently through a false letter or report, they had been led to believe that the Day of the Lord had already come, and they were now in the predicted time of trouble from which they had been assured they would be delivered in I Thessalonians 5. In correcting this misunderstanding, the apostle definitely states that the Day of the Lord cannot come until apostasy of a special character takes place as defined in II Thessalonians 2:3, 4: "Let no man deceive you by any means: for that day shall not come, except there come a falling away first, and that man of sin be revealed, the son of perdition; who opposeth and exalteth himself above all that is called God, or that is worshipped; so that he as God sitteth in the temple of God, shewing himself that he is God."

According to this revelation, the Day of the Lord which apparently follows the rapture of the church cannot come, that is, cannot fulfill its predicted character until there be "a falling away first" or, as it may be literally translated, "a departure first." It has been debated whether this departure refers to the departure of the church as indicated in the rapture or whether the traditional interpretation that it refers to a departure from the faith should be in view. If it refers to the rapture, it is an explicit statement that the rapture must occur before the Day of the Lord and it constitutes a support of the pretribulational position. If it refers to the departure from faith, i.e., apostasy, it teaches that the Day of the Lord cannot come until the man of sin be revealed, a person described as "the son of perdition; who opposeth and exalteth himself above all that is called God, or that is worshipped; so that he as God sitteth in the temple of God, shewing himself that he is God" (II Thessalonians 2:3, 4). Most expositors refer this description to the first beast of Revelation 13, the one described as the coming world ruler who will be worshiped by all men. Some refer it to the second beast of Revelation 13, that is, the false prophet who will be the religious head of the world in that day. In either case the reference is to a period between the rapture of the church and the second coming of Christ to the earth, a period described by our Lord as a time of great tribulation.

The apostasy here described, while a ·culmination of the apostasy which characterizes the end of the church age, has the peculiar character of centering in a man who claims that he is God and demands that the entire world worship him. The description corresponds to that found in Revelation 13 where the world ruler is described as one who blasphemes God, who has power for forty-two months, the exact length of the great tribulation, who makes war with the saints, who has power over all kindred, tongues, and nations, and whom all that dwell upon the earth shall worship (Revelation 13:5-8).

When the rapture of the church takes place, every true Christian will be caught up out of the world. Those who are within the professing church who are left behind are unsaved and without real redemption in Christ. There is little to hinder their progression into the utter apostasy described for this period which is completely devoid of Biblical truth. The false religion of that day will be inspired of Satan, and culminates in the worship of a man who blasphemes God and all that is called Christian. The character of apostasy before and after the rapture therefore stands in sharp contrast, though in some sense the apostasy following the rapture builds upon that which has preceded it.

As will be brought out in later discussion, apostasy in this period takes two forms. First, that which has the semblance of Christianity and is the culmination of the movement toward a world church, as will be characteristic of the first part of the period between the rapture and the second coming. Second, the final stage of apostasy will follow, which will be that predicted in II Thessalonians 2 and Revelation 13, namely, the worship of Satan's man who will be both the political dictator of the world and the object of its worship as God. The superchurch foreshadowed in Revelation 13 is seen also in Revelation 17 in the symbolism of the harlot sitting upon the beast. The final state is that of the worship of the world ruler who has destroyed the superchurch in favor of the worship of himself (Revelation 17:16).

PROPHECIES OF THE END OF THE CHURCH AGE FULFILLED

The important conclusion which may be reached upon a careful study of prophecies dealing with the end of the church age is that all that is necessary before the rapture has been fulfilled, and that we can confidently await the coming of the Lord for His church as the next step in the fulfillment of prophecy relating to the church. There is a sense in which this has always been true inasmuch as these prophecies were to some extent fulfilled even in the first century. With the passing of the years, however, the trend has been irresistibly in the direction foreshadowed by these prophecies and today the situation is clearly parallel to that which is anticipated in the great prophecies of Paul, Peter and John.

In the Middle Ages, the ignorance and unbelief of the masses as well as the blindness of the church could be traced in part to a lack of dissemination of ideas. In a modern world, however, where communications have reached a new peak with multiplied thousands of books and other publications supplemented by radio and television, there is less excuse today than ever before in the history of the world for unbelief. To a large portion of the world, at least, the facts are available for those who wish to investigate. In the face of such modern conveniences and opportunity, unbelief is all the more startling because, humanly speaking, God has no other device than that of proclamation of the truth.

The world today is responsible not because the truth is inaccessible but because they have turned away from it deliberately. There is no recourse in such a situation but divine judgment. The best efforts of the evangelical church are falling far short in keeping up with the increasing birth rate, much less countering the avalanche of unbelief and ridicule which expresses the world's attitude toward divine revelation. The stage is therefore set for a demonstration of the power of God, first in the period of judgment preceding the second coming, and then climaxing in the second coming of Christ and the gathering of the nations before the bar of divine justice.

For the true church, it means that the days of its pilgrimage may be coming fast to a close. On the one hand, this calls for expenditure of every effort to snatch as brands from the burning those who have not yet come to Christ. On the other hand, the hope of His soon return should constitute both a comfort and a challenge to be "always abounding in the work of the Lord" (I Corinthians 15:58) and to purity of life and motive (I John 3:3).

CHAPTER V

THE RESURRECTION OF THE CHURCH

The doctrine of the resurrection of the dead in Christ and the translation of the living church is one of the prominent aspects of the earlier epistles of Paul. In I and II Thessalonians, which are probably the first two books of the Bible to come from the pen of Paul, the coming of the Lord is mentioned in every chapter. In addition to the classic revelation of the resurrection and translation of the church in I Thessalonians 4:13 − 5:11, the subject is mentioned in I Thessalonians 1:10; 2:19; 3:13; 5:23; II Thessalonians 2:1-12; 3:5. In addition there seems to be a clear reference to Christ coming to establish His kingdom in II Thessalonians 1:7-10.

The ministry of the Apostle Paul to the Thessalonians is remarkable in many particulars. According to Acts 17:1-10, Paul accompanied by Silas and Timothy had ministered in Thessalonica "three sabbath days" involving at the least fifteen days and at the most twenty-seven days. In this comparatively brief period of time, their ministry had been so effective that a small group of believers was formed. Paul had instructed them in the rudiments of the Christian faith, including the doctrine of the first coming of Christ with its gospel message and the doctrine of the second coming of Christ attended by the resurrection of the dead and the rapture of the living. In addition, he had also taught them concerning election (I Thessalonians 1:4), the Holy Spirit (1:5, 6; 4:8; 5:19), the doctrine of the assurance of salvation (1:5), the doctrine of the Trinity, Father, Son, and Holy Spirit (1:1, 5, 6, etc.), the doctrine of conversion and Christian walk (1:9; 2:12; 4:1), sanctification (4:3; 5:23), the coming Day of the Lord (5:1-9), and the nature of man (5:23). Though all of these doctrines may not have been explained fully or technically, it is apparent that the Thessalonians knew something about them, for Paul seems to appeal to previous knowledge as he expounds these subjects in I Thessalonians.

The coming of the Lord is one of the central themes of the Thessalonian epistles. In I Thessalonians 1:10 they were exhorted "to wait for his Son from heaven, whom he raised from the dead, even Jesus, which delivered us from the wrath to come." In I Thessalonians 2:19, exulting over the wonderful spiritual progress made by the Thessalonians and their testimony before the world, Paul asked the question, "For what is our hope, or joy, or crown of rejoicing?" He answered, "Are not even ye in the presence of our Lord Jesus Christ at his coming? For ye are our glory and joy" (I Thessalonians 2:10, 20).

In I Thessalonians 3:13, after exhorting them "to increase and abound in love one toward another and toward all men" (I Thessalonians 3:12), he held before them the goal of holiness at the coming of the Lord. "To the end he may stablish your hearts unblameable in holiness before God, even our Father, at the coming of our Lord Jesus Christ with all his saints" (I Thessalonians 3:13). In a similar way he challenged them to realize the fullness of spiritual attainment in the Christian life and expressed the prayer that "the very God of peace sanctify you holy; and I pray God your whole spirit and soul and body be preserved blameless unto the coming of our Lord Jesus Christ." It is obvious from these references that the Thessalonians had not only been taught the coming of the Lord, but it was a prominent factor in Paul's exhortations to them for holy living and faithful witness. Here as throughout the Pauline epistles, the rapture and translation of the church is viewed as an imminent event and one for which Christians should be constantly ready.

After Paul had left Thessalonica, being forced to flee because of the persecution which threatened his life, he sent Timothy back to Thessalonica. This is indicated in I Thessalonians 3:2, where he declared his purpose for Timothy "to establish you and to comfort you concerning your faith." Timothy after ministering to them was instructed to bring back tidings to Paul. Upon rejoining Paul, Timothy informed him of the steadfast faith of the Thessalonian Christians. They had stood fast in the midst of affliction and persecution in unwavering joy of the Spirit with the result that their testimony had reached not only to all Macedonia and Achaia, but even to more distant points, as Paul indicates in I Thessalonians 1:6-8. With the good tidings Timothy brought back to Paul were several questions the Thessalonian Christians had asked which were beyond Timothy's understanding. These are answered by the apostle in this epistle.

One of the important questions concerned the relationship of the translation of the living church to the resurrection of Christians who had died. It seems apparent that this issue had not been raised while Paul was with them at Thessalonica as they had not faced the possibility that some of their number would die before the Lord came. In the short time since Paul's departure, however, some of the Thessalonians had gone to be with the Lord, possibly as a result of persecution. Their question was whether these dead in Christ would be raised at the same time the living church was raptured, or whether this resurrection would take place at some later time.

It may be presuming too much to assume that the Thessalonians understood clearly the sequence of end-time events including the order of the rapture, followed by the time of tribulation, and climaxing in the second coming of Christ to establish His kingdom. The question, however, fits naturally into this context, inasmuch as they did not question the fact of the resurrection of the dead in Christ, but only the time when this would take place. It would seem from this that they did not have in mind, what the post-tribulationist takes for granted, that the rapture and the resurrection both occur in connection with Christ's coming to establish His kingdom.

Their understanding of prophecy presumed a series of events preceding Christ's coming to establish His kingdom. They probably would not have asked the question if they had not had in mind something equivalent to the present position of pretribulationists who hold that the rapture precedes the tribulation. Specifically, they may have wondered whether the resurrection of the church would take place in connection with Christ's establishment of His kingdom, even though the translation of living saints preceded the tribulation. In answer to this question, the classic passage beginning in I Thessalonians 4:13 constitutes the divine exposition of this important aspect of the Christian hope relating to the Lord's return.

THE COMFORT OF THE LORD'S RETURN
I Thessalonians 4:13, 14

In the introduction to the revelation concerning the rapture, the apostle begins by stating, "But I would not have you to be ignorant, brethren, concerning them which are asleep, that ye sorrow not, even as others which have no hope." In twentieth-century Christianity, it has become fashionable in some quarters to downgrade prophecy as an unimportant aspect of Biblical revelation. The plea is often made that because of the controversial character of eschatology and the fact that there is widespread difference of opinion on some important facts relating to the future, the best policy for the church would be to emphasize other aspects of Christian doctrine and to be relatively silent in the area of prophecy.

The Apostle Paul and the early church did not share this point of view, for the hope of the church and especially the hope of the Lord's return were large factors in their faith. Here the apostle rather bluntly states that he does not want the Thessalonian Christians to be ignorant concerning the facts which he is now going to expound. Instead, they should have a real hope, and he is zealous that they know the details which pertain to it.

His reason for instructing them is a practical one, namely, "that ye sorrow not, even as others which have no hope." The hopelessness of the unbeliever embodied in the expression, "no hope," is in dramatic contrast to the bright expectation of the Christian looking for the Lord. It is important to note that the unbeliever has no hope at all, that there is no second chance, no probation in the eternal state, no purgatory from which he will finally emerge acceptable to God. The future of the unbeliever is one of stark despair. The Christian, however, has a wonderful hope which Paul proceeds to unfold. This hope relates not only to the believer's personal destiny but also involves His loved ones in Christ who are described as "asleep," a softened expression for death, having implicit in it the idea that a Christian will awake at the time of the resurrection.

Not only is the Christian hope a wonderful comfort in the time of bereavement, but it is also a fundamental aspect of Christian faith. In I Thessalonians 4:14, Paul states, "If we believe that Jesus died and rose again, even so them also which sleep in Jesus will God bring with him." Here the truth of the Lord's return is tied in with the indispensable essentials of the faith, namely, that Jesus died and rose again. It should be clear to all students of Scripture that, while Christians may differ in their understanding of certain aspects of prophecy as well as in other areas of doctrine, there is an irreducible minimum to a true Christian theology apart from which Christianity loses its meanings and significance. The deity of Christ and His work on the cross in that He both died for our sins and rose again is such a central doctrine. Faith in Christ becomes meaningless unless it includes this aspect of confidence in His person and His work. This, according to I Corinthians 15:3, 4, is the Gospel of salvation and the faith of every true believer, as indicated in the words of Romans 10:9, "If thou shalt confess with thy mouth the Lord Jesus, and shalt believe in thine heart that God hath raised Him from the dead, thou shalt be saved."

The clause, "if we believe," does not introduce an element of uncertainty but refers to the fact of faith, namely, that which is absolutely true. The thought is, "because we believe that Jesus died and rose again," we can have certain hope. Just as surely as one accepts the death of Christ for one's sin and His bodily resurrection from the grave, so also one can accept with equal assurance the wonderful truth of the coming of the Lord and the resurrection of those who have died in Christ. Christian hope is an outgrowth of the historic faith of the church in what has already been accomplished in the death and resurrection of Christ.

The expression, "them also which sleep in Jesus will God bring with him," refers to the fact that when Christ returns from heaven, He will be accompanied by the dead in Christ. When Christians experience physical death on earth, their bodies are laid in the grave, but their souls and spirits go to be with the Lord. As Paul wrote later to the Corinthians, "to be absent from the body" is "to be present with the Lord" (II Corinthians 5:8). On the occasion of His return to the earth and in anticipation of the resurrection of the bodies of the saints, the Lord brings with Him the souls and the spirits of these who have died in Christ. The thought is that in the resurrection their souls and spirits will re-enter their bodies which will be restored and transformed.

RESURRECTION BEFORE TRANSLATION
I Thessalonians 4:15, 16

The apostle now proceeds to answer their question as to whether the translation of the living church will precede that of the resurrection of the dead in Christ. He states plainly that the translation of the living will not precede the resurrection of the dead: "For this we say unto you by the word of the Lord, that we which are alive and remain unto the coming of the Lord shall not prevent them which are asleep" (I Thessalonians 4:15). The revelation is introduced by the unusual phrase, "by the word of the Lord." By this should be understood that Paul had a special revelation from God on this point which preceded the writing of this Scripture. In some cases, inspiration coincides with the revelation of the truth in that the truth is contained in what is being written even though it was not previously completely understood. In this case, however, the apostle had a special revelation from God which he is now recording for the benefit of the Thessalonian church. The revelation of the order of events as given to the apostle is that the resurrection of the saints, who have died in Christ, shall occur first, and that the translation of the living saints should occur next. This is explained in the verses which follow.

Paul, in revealing the order of events, declares, "For the Lord himself shall descend from heaven with a shout, with the voice of the archangel, and with the trump of God: and the dead in Christ shall rise first" (I Thessalonians 4:16). A threefold event takes place in connection with the resurrection of the dead in Christ. First, the Lord Himself shall descend from heaven with a shout. This involves the descent of the Lord from the third heaven or the immediate presence of God in the atmospheric heaven. Upon His arrival in the earthly scene, the Lord gives "a shout." The particular Greek word used by Paul for "shout" has the meaning of a military command. No explanation is given as to the exact character of this command, but it undoubtedly refers to the resurrection of the dead and possibly includes the translation of the living saints.

At the tomb of Lazarus in John 11, it is recorded that Christ going to the tomb had cried with a loud voice, "Lazarus, come forth" (John 11:43). At the command of

Christ, Lazarus came forth still bound in grave clothes and his face covered with a napkin. To the astounded witnesses, Christ issued the order, "Loose him, and let him go" (John 11:44). This incident is in keeping with the declaration of Christ in John 5 that the dead shall be raised at His command.

In John 5:25, Christ predicted, "The hour is coming, and now is, when the dead shall hear the voice of the Son of God: and they that hear shall live." This apparently refers to those who are spiritually dead but still alive physically who shall hear the voice of the Son of God and receive eternal life. In commenting on this, He goes on to add in John 5:28, 29, "Marvel not at this: for the hour is coming, in the which all that are in the grave shall hear his voice, and shall go forth; they that have done good, unto the resurrection of life; and they that have done evil, unto the resurrection of damnation." In I Thessalonians 4, there is a partial fulfillment of this resurrection of life.

It should be clear from many other Scriptures that all the dead are not raised at the time of the resurrection of the dead in Christ. This is a resurrection of life in contrast to the resurrection of damnation which occurs over a thousand years later, as indicated in Revelation 20. At the voice of the Lord, however, the dead in Christ hear His voice and rise. This selective resurrection is described in Philippians 3:11 as "the resurrection out from among the dead" (literally translated). Just as the resurrection of Lazarus was selective in that Lazarus' name was called and only he was restored to life, so in this resurrection only the dead in Christ hear the voice and rise in answer to the summons. Christ has authority to raise all the dead and ultimately will use this authority, but here the command is addressed only to those who qualify for this particular resurrection.

Accompanying the shout of command which the Lord Himself issued is the voice of the archangel, who is called Michael five times in the Scripture (Daniel 10:13, 21; 12:1;

Jude 9; Revelation 12:7). Only here in the Bible is he referred to as the archangel without the name, and only in Jude 9 is both the name and his title of archangel mentioned. Michael has the honor of being head of the holy angels, the leader of the forces of righteousness against the forces of Satan. Some intimation of the angelic struggle with the forces of darkness is indicated in other passages of Scripture such as Daniel 10, Ephesians 6:11-18, and Revelation 12:7. Michael was not only the leader of the angelic throng, but also the special champion of Israel as shown in his relationship to Daniel in Daniel 10 and the express statement of Daniel 12:1 that he was "the great prince which standeth with the children of thy people." The introduction of the voice of the archangel at this point has suggested to some that not only the dead in Christ, that is, the saints of the present age since Pentecost, but also Israel and all the saints of the Old Testament will be included in the rapture.

A careful examination of the references pertaining to the resurrection of Israel, however, seem to point to the conclusion that Israel will be raised at the end of the tribulation rather than at its beginning. This has led some to accept the post-tribulation interpretation of the rapture on the basis that if Israel and the church are raised at the same time, and Israel is not raised until after the tribulation, the church also must endure the tribulation before experiencing resurrection and translation.

There is no reason, however, to confuse the resurrection of the church with the resurrection of Israel as these seem to be two separate events. According to Daniel 12:1, apparently at the time of the end of the great tribulation described in Daniel 11:36-45, Michael shall stand up and there shall be a "time of trouble, such as never was since there was a nation even to that same time." The deliverance of the people of Israel will then take place as indicated in the phrase, "at that time my people shall be delivered, everyone that shall be found written in the book." The deliverance obviously has to do with Israelites still living on the earth at the end of the tribulation. Immediately following this revelation, however, in Daniel 12:2, mention is made of the resurrection of Israel, "and many of them that sleep in the dust of the earth shall awake, some to everlasting life, and some to shame and everlasting contempt." Like the passage in John 5:28, 29, the resurrection of all men is included here as a fact even though that resurrection, according to other Scriptures, will take place in stages. The important point, however, in Daniel's revelation is that resurrection of Israel is associated with the deliverance of Israelites living on the earth at the end of the tribulation. Apparently the deliverance of living Israelites is going to coincide in time with the resurrection of Israelites who have died but who are worthy of everlasting life.

In view of the fact that the Scriptures clearly indicate that there will be a resurrection of the tribulation saints at the end of the tribulation period (Revelation 20:4-6), it is probable that the resurrection of Old Testament saints including the resurrection of righteous Israel will take place at the same time in preparation for the reign of Christ on earth in which some of the resurrected Israelites such as David will be prominent. The resurrection of the "dead in Christ" is a different event including only those baptized into the body of Christ, i.e., the saints of the present age.

The voice of the archangel in I Thessalonians 4:16 may be best interpreted as a shout of triumph. It is understandable that Michael, as a leader of the forces of righteousness through many millenniums, should rejoice in this great demonstration of the power and the grace of God. In spite of all that Satan had been able to do in thwarting the work and testimony of God through the centuries as witnessed in the failure of the professing church, here at long last is the church perfect and complete, a testimony to the certainty of God's divine purposes and a witness to His grace for all eternity to come. The voice of the command of the Lord is therefore accompanied by the archangel's voice of triumph.

The third stage of the events described in I Thessalonians 4:16 is that of the sounding of the trump of God. According to the context, this trump has to do with the resurrection of the dead in Christ and the translation of the living and therefore should not be confused with other trumps in Scripture. In the Old Testament, trumpets were used on a great variety of occasions and signaled various things in connection with the Word of God. In the first century the trump also was a familiar sound. It was used by the Roman soldiers for many different purposes. They were aroused in the morning by trumpets, were assembled for the march of that day by another trumpet, and the forward march was signaled by still another trumpet.

The expression here, "the trump of God," must therefore be considered a parallel to the last trump of I Corinthians 15:52, but should not be confused with other trumpets in the New Testament. In contrast to the seven trumps of angels in Revelation 8:2-9, 21; 11:15-18, this is a trump of God, a trump of grace, a trump of triumph, and a trump pertaining to the righteous dead and living saints. The trumpets of Revelation by contrast are trumps sounded by angels related to judgment poured out upon a Christ-rejecting world and signaling various catastrophes which were a form of the divine chastisement of the world in future time of tribulation. Other than the word *trump*, there is no relationship between these two events as they announce an entirely different aspect of the divine program.

The trump of God here should also not be confused with the trumpet mentioned in Matthew 24:31, though there are some similarities. The trumpet of Matthew has to do with the gathering of the elect from one end of heaven to another. Mark's Gospel adds that it also includes the uttermost part of the earth. Some have taken the elect in view in Matthew as the elect nation Israel, while others refer it to the elect of all ages, but no resurrection or translation is in view in either case. It is simply that the elect are gathered from all areas and brought together. Such a gathering will take place at the time of the second coming of Christ to establish His earthly kingdom; but those gathered include not only the resurrected and translated church, the resurrected saints of the Old Testament, and the resurrected saints of the tribulation, but extends to those who are living on earth at that time. In a word, it is all the elect in Matthew 24, whereas in I Thessalonians 4, it seems to refer only to the dead in Christ and those who are living at that time.

The expression, "the dead in Christ," is most distinctive because the phrase, "in Christ," is used in the Bible only to refer to saints who lived in the period beginning at Pentecost. The term is never used of Israel or of Gentile believers in the Old Testament, nor is it ever used of saints in the tribulation time, though Christ representatively died on the cross for all men with a special view to the salvation of the elect. The church enjoys a special relationship embodied in the phrase, "in Christ," which is a result of the baptism of the Holy Spirit (I Corinthians 12:13). It is this relationship which makes the church a distinct body of saints and marks the limits of the inclusion of the resurrection that is in view in I Thessalonians 4:16.

At the threefold event of the shout of the Lord, the voice of the archangel, and the trump of God, Paul reveals that the dead in Christ shall rise first. In other words, the first response to this great event is that the dead in Christ shall be raised. As will be considered later in the discussion of I Corinthians 15:51, 52, they will receive a resurrection body comparable to that of Christ Himself (I John 3:2), a body which will be holy, immortal, and incorruptible, suited for the presence of the holy, infinite God.

THE TRANSLATION OF THE LIVING CHURCH
I Thessalonians 4:17

Immediately following the resurrection of the dead in Christ, the living saints are declared in I Thessalonians 4:17 to be caught up to meet the Lord with the resurrected saints, "Then we which are alive and remain shall

be caught up together with them in the clouds, to meet
the Lord in the air: and so shall we ever be with the Lord."
It is obvious from this description that the time gap between the resurrection of the dead and the translation of
the living is momentary. They are "caught up together."
The answer to the question which had originally been pro-
posed by the Thessalonians is, therefore, clear. Living Christians will not have to wait for the resurrection of their
loved ones for, as a matter of fact, they will precede them
momentarily and having been raised from the dead will be
joined by the living church which is also caught up to be
with the Lord.

The expression, "caught up together," is the Biblical
source of the word *rapture*. The Latin translation of "caught
up" is *rapturo*, from which the English word *rapture* is derived. Though often the word *rapture* means to be carried
away with joy, here it refers to a bodily "snatching up,"
that is, the bodily removal of the living church from the
earth and meeting the Lord in the air.

It is clear from this passage that the living church
at the time will never experience death. Such a possibility
of passing into heaven without dying is anticipated in the
translation of Enoch and Elijah in the Old Testament, the
only exception to the normal rule that resurrection is preceded by death. Even Christ died on the cross and followed
the order of death first, and a later resurrection. Here a
whole generation of saints will pass into the immediate
presence of the Lord without experiencing physical death.

The expression, "in the clouds," is without the article
in the Greek, and some have interpreted this as referring
not to atmospheric clouds but to the living saints appearing in great numbers as a cloud. In a similar way, there
is reference in Hebrews 12:1 to "so great a cloud of witnesses." It is probable, however, that just as atmospheric
clouds received the Lord when He ascended into heaven
(Acts 1:9) and as He will come in "the clouds of heaven"
at His return to the earth, so here also at the rapture the

church will be enveloped by the atmospheric heavens and thus be taken out of sight of men on earth. There is no indication, however, that residents of earth will be able to see the church thus raptured.

The place of meeting of the church with the Lord is specified as "in the air." This makes plain that this passage does not refer to physical death as some have attempted to interpret it. The passage itself contains a sharp contrast between the dead in Christ who are resurrected and living saints who are caught up to meet the Lord. In the case of the death of Christians, their souls and spirits go to the third heaven. There is no evidence whatever that they are met by angels or by the Lord or by anyone else. Here, however, the entire company caught up at one moment is to be assembled to meet the Lord in the air.

Some have attempted to explain this expression, "in the air," as referring to the state of the church throughout the tribulation, namely, that the church is in the air, rather than on earth, but not in the third heaven. Such does not seem to be the case. According to John 14:1-3, when the Lord comes for His own, He comes to take them to the place prepared in heaven, i.e., the third heaven or the immediate presence of God. The Father's house is where God characteristically resides and this apparently is the destination of the church after meeting the Lord in the air. When the Lord returns to earth later to establish His millennial kingdom, He comes from the third heaven (Revelation 19:11). In any case, the comforting assurance is given, "so shall we ever be with the Lord." From this time on, where the Lord is, so will be the church. There will be no separation either physically or spiritually but perfect fellowship and perfect harmony. Though the apostle does not state it in so many words, it is also implicit in the passage that we will also be with our loved ones in Christ forever and that our separation from them also will cease on the occasion of the rapture of the church. This blessed prospect is the hope of the church and the reason why

Paul exhorts them to "sorrow not even as others which have no hope."

THE COMMAND TO COMFORT
I Thessalonians 4:18

The tremendous revelation concerning the coming of Christ both for the dead in Christ and living saints culminates in the exhortation, "Wherefore comfort one another with these words." Here again the apostle firmly takes the position that prophecy is a practical truth concerning which Christians should not be ignorant, and which should inspire hope and assurance, as well as comfort for those in bereavement. The word translated "comfort" implies, however, much more than simply help in times of bereavement. It has the idea of help in general, of exhortation, of urging on in the task, and of encouragement. The subject of the rapture should be included not only in the teaching and the preaching ministry of the church, but also in the conversation of Christians. They were to comfort one another with these words in times of special stress and strain when the cares of earth and its trials seemingly become burdensome. In such an hour, the comfort of the Lord's return is indescribably wonderful.

The fact that this truth is extended here to those who have lost loved ones is another indication that the Thessalonian Christians were expecting the Lord's return any day. There does not seem to be any indication in this passage that they were extended this hope only as something which could be realized after passing through the indescribable persecution of the great tribulation. Such a comfort would be tenuous at best, as the Scriptures seem to indicate the great majority of those saved in the great tribulation will perish before the second coming. If the hope of the Thessalonian Christians was endurance through this period with the possibility of survival and rapture at its end, it would not have been the comfort and hope which Paul was now expressing. In contrast to this, there is not any indication in this passage that their hope was anything other than an imminent hope. They are not warned that they must go through this period first. Instead, they have extended to them the wonderful hope that any day the Lord may come and that they may be caught up in His presence with their loved ones raised from the dead. Not only is the matter of tribulation never interposed in a rapture passage, such as this is, but in the revelation following in chapter 5 they are assured that the troubles predicted of the end times are not part of their schedule in God's program.

THE DAY OF THE LORD IMMINENT
I Thessalonians 5:1-3

Immediately following this great passage on the rapture of the church is a further discussion obviously arising from the rapture doctrine, namely, the question of the times and seasons when end-time events will have their fulfillment. In the opening verses of chapter 5, the apostle reveals that the Day of the Lord will come as a thief in the night i.e., unexpectedly and without warning: "But of the times and the season, brethren, ye have no need that I write unto you. For yourselves know perfectly that the day of the Lord so cometh as a thief in the night. For when they shall say, Peace and safety; then sudden destruction cometh upon them, as travail upon a woman with child; and they shall not escape."

In his discussion of the doctrine of the rapture, he states that he does not need to write to them concerning the times, that is, the general times, or the seasons, that is, the particular times which relate to the coming of the Lord. This is in contrast to I Thessalonians 4:13 where he states that he does not want them to be ignorant concerning the details of the prophecy concerning the rapture. Here he tells them that they already know the facts concerning the times and seasons, namely, that the coming of the Day of the Lord is imminent.

The expression, "The Day of the Lord," is a common one in both the Old and New Testament and seems to refer to that extended period of time in which the Lord will deal directly with human sin in various forms of divine judgment. The Old Testament commonly speaks of the Day of the Lord as a period characterized as "a day of darkness and gloominess, a day of clouds and of thick darkness" (Joel 2:2), "when all the inhabitants of the land tremble" (Joel 2:1), when there will be warfare and destruction of the land (Joel 2:3-9), and when "the earth shall quake. . . ; the heavens shall tremble: the sun and the moon shall be dark, and the stars shall withdraw their shining" (Joel 2:10). As Joel explains, "The day of the LORD is great and very terrible; and who can abide it?" It is, therefore, the period of divine judgment preceding the return of Christ to the earth. According to Zephaniah, however, it will also include, following the period of the "day of wrath" (Zephaniah 1:14-18), a time of rejoicing which will follow the day of judgment (Zephaniah 3:14-20). From these various passages, it has been concluded that the Day of the Lord includes not only the time of tribulation subsequent to the rapture but also the entire thousand-year reign of Christ on earth.

In the perspective of the Thessalonian church, they were living in the day of grace, the present dispensation in which God is gathering out both Jew and Gentile to form one body of the church. When the rapture occurs, this work of God will be brought to its close and the Day of the Lord will begin. Though some of its major events would not take place immediately, the period in general would extend from the rapture until the end of the millennium. This in turn would be followed by the Day of God according to II Peter 3:12, 13 beginning with the destruction of the heaven and the earth with fire and the creation of a new heaven and a new earth. The destruction, therefore, predicted by Peter in II Peter 3:10 as occurring in the Day of the Lord actually is the boundary between the Day of the Lord and the Day of God. Putting these facts together, the prophetic perspective therefore is for three general periods, the first the day of grace or the present age, next the Day of the Lord or the Day of Jehovah from the rapture to the end of the millennium, and then the Day of God or the eternal day. The coming of the Day of the Lord, therefore, is coincident with the rapture itself and for this reason the apostle discusses its arrival as if it were one and the same as the rapture of the church itself. Just as the Day of the Lord would come as a thief, so also the rapture. Though expected by those who believe in the doctrine of the rapture, it would come upon the earth in their state of total unpreparedness.

The time of the coming of the Day of the Lord is described in verse 3 as a period when the world is going to be saying, "Peace and safety." The world at that time will be considering ways and means of achieving world peace and safety apart from Christ and His kingdom of peace and righteousness. There is some indication that in the period immediately following the rapture, there will be concerted effort on the part of the world to solve the problems created by an atomic age and to do what is humanly possible — to achieve a world peace. It is in the midst of this that sudden destruction will come upon them.

This sudden destruction will be preceded by the rapture and the beginning of the period in which the sudden destruction will take place. It does not mean that the world will be destroyed immediately after the rapture of the church or at the beginning of the Day of the Lord, but the rapture of the church having already occurred, they are now plunged into the maelstrom of the judgments of God to be inflicted at the end of the age. Their situation is described as similar to that of travail coming upon a woman with child. Though the birth of a child can in general be predicted and anticipated, the exact hour is unknown. Their time of trouble, however, is just as inevitable as the ultimate birth of a child. The sad pronouncement is made, "They shall not escape." In contrast to the church which will escape, because they will be caught up to be with the Lord before this time of trouble begins, those who are left behind are inevitably doomed to pass through this time of unprecedented trouble.

THE CHURCH NOT IN DARKNESS
I Thessalonians 5:4, 5

The statement, "But ye, brethren, are not in darkness, that that day should overtake you as a thief," contrasts the position of a Christian to that of one who is an unbeliever in that day. The world at the present time is in spiritual darkness which will be followed by the Day of the Lord when the rapture occurs. By contrast, the Christian is living today in the knowledge of divine revelation. Though the church also does not know the precise date of the rapture, it is not unexpected as in the case of the unbeliever. Because of the peculiar fact that the church is going to be caught up to be with the Lord at the time the Day of the Lord begins, the Day of the Lord will not overtake the church as a thief at all and the church will lose nothing when the Day of the Lord comes.

In verse 5, the contrast between the Christian and the unbeliever is continued, "Ye are all the children of light, and the children of the day: we are not of the night, nor of darkness." The apostle reassured the Thessalonians that they are all the children of light, meaning by that all who were in the Thessalonian church. Knowing them personally, as he does, he is assured of their individual salvation as he had previously indicated in I Thessalonians 1:4-10. Christians are described as living in the light of divine revelation and the grace of God. In the latter part of the verse the apostle includes himself when he states, "we are not of the night, nor of darkness." They have the wonderful position of living in the daylight rather than in the night of unbelief and ignorance. The spiritual darkness which characterizes the unbelieving world is going to extend into the Day of the Lord even as the spiritual light which is presently possessed by the church is going to merge into the eternal light of being in the presence of the Lord. The absolute contrast between the believer and the unbeliever, established not only by the fact of their difference in relation to light but also their destiny relative to the Day of

the Lord, reassured the Thessalonians that they do not need
to fear this future time of trouble. It is most important to
note that the apostle does not in any wise indicate that they
will enter the day of the Lord and the judgments which it
will bring upon the world. Rather, they have nothing to fear
for the Lord is coming for them.

EXHORTATION TO WATCH AND BE SOBER
I Thessalonians 5:6-8

The fact that the Thessalonians and all other true believers are children of the light involves not only a wonderful hope but a present responsibility. Here, as throughout
the Word of God, prophecy is not viewed simply as something to be admired and looked forward to but a revelation from God which emphasizes present duty and responsibility. In view of the fact that they are children of the
light, he exhorts them in verse 6, "Therefore let us not
sleep, as do others; but let us watch and be sober." It is
characteristic for the world to sleep at night and unbelievers
are spiritually asleep even in the present day of grace. By
contrast, however, the Christian living in the atmosphere of
spiritual light should be alert and should be watching for
the coming of the Lord in contrast to drunkenness which
often characterizes the world as they celebrate in the night.
The Christians should watch and be sober. Concerning unbelievers, in verse 7 he states, "For they that sleep sleep in
the night; and they that be drunken are drunken in the
night." The world, characteristically, is either asleep or
drunken in the night. In relation to their spiritual situation,
they are stupefied either by sleep or by drunkenness and are
unaware of their terrible danger. In exhorting the Christian
to watch, it is noteworthy that Paul does not hold before
them signs such as would normally be included in a revelation concerning Christ's coming to establish His kingdom as illustrated in the Olivet discourse, Matthew 24-25.
Here they are exhorted to watch for the coming of the
Lord itself and not for preceding signs. The idea is that

the coming of the Lord is imminent and an event that they could expect at any time.

Again applying the truth that they are in the day and should be sober, he elaborates on what ought to characterize their life and testimony. They should "be sober, putting on the breastplate of faith, hope, and love" in order of experience. The Christian life begins with faith which opens the windows of the mind and heart and lets the light of the Word of God shine in. Faith is not only the means by which God pours the blessings of grace upon the believers, but it also is the breastplate, that which protects from Satan and the evil world. Through faith also comes love, both the love of God and love for fellow Christians which is a fruit of the Holy Spirit. In view of the fact that Christians will spend eternity in fellowship one with the other as well as in the presence of God, they are exhorted to begin that love relationship which is the unmistakable mark of a disciple of Jesus Christ. As Christ said in the upper room, "By this shall all men know that ye are my disciples, if ye have love one for another" (John 13:35).

The final piece of armor to protect the Christian is the helmet which is symbolically the hope of salvation. The Christian not only has salvation in the present tense in that he knows that he belongs to the Lord and is experiencing the Lord's delivering power, but the Christian also has the expectation of future deliverance such as will be his at the rapture of the church. The figure of a helmet as a type of salvation is also mentioned in the later epistle of Paul to the Ephesians (6:17) where the spiritual realities which are the possession of the Christian are described also in terms of armor. The Christian is to enter fully into what God has provided for his present pilgrim walk as well as to look for that ultimate deliverance which will bring him into the presence of the Lord.

OUR APPOINTMENT TO SALVATION, NOT TO WRATH
I Thessalonians 5:9-11

By way of summary of what the apostle has been discussing in the preceding verses of this chapter, he concludes in verse 9, "For God hath not appointed us to wrath, but to obtain salvation by our Lord Jesus Christ." This is a categorical denial that the church will go through the tribulation which is described as a day of wrath (Revelation 6:17). The whole argument of this section is that the Christian will not enter the Day of the Lord, that he belongs to a different day, that he is looking for the coming of the Lord and not for the Day of the Lord. The idea sometimes advanced that the Christian will be preserved through the tribulation and in this sense will be kept from the wrath of God is beside the point. It is not that the Christian will be kept from wrath which, of course, is always true under all circumstances even if a Christian is martyred; but it is rather that this is not our appointment. The characteristics of the day of wrath, unfolded in the book of Revelation and anticipated in prophecies concerning the Day of the Lord in the Old Testament, reveal forms of divine judgment which inevitably will afflict the entire human race. War, pestilence, famine, earthquakes, and stars falling from heaven are not by their nature selective but are almost universal in their application. This is not the Christian's appointment who is looking for the coming of the Lord at the rapture. It is rather that our expectation is one of obtaining salvation by our Lord Jesus Christ. The salvation that is here viewed as in verse 8, where it is called the "hope of salvation," is salvation in its total aspect, not simply salvation from the guilt of sin or deliverance from the present evil world, but that salvation which will be made complete when we stand in the presence of the Lord.

The deliverance which is thus provided does not stem from human attainment and righteousness but is based upon the work of Christ on the cross. This the apostle points out clearly in I Thessalonians 5:10 when in reference to the Lord Jesus Christ he states, "Who died for us, that, whether we wake or sleep, we should live together with him." He is referring in this verse to the contrast between those who have died in Christ and those who will be living at the time

Christ comes. Those who wake are those who are still alive, who have not died and who are waiting the Lord at His coming. Those who sleep are those who have fallen asleep in Jesus. Both classifications are going to live together with Christ forever once the rapture of the church has taken place.

As in the close of chapter 4, so here after the discussion of the Day of the Lord and the Christian's deliverance from it, he closes with the exhortation in I Thessalonians 5:11, "Wherefore comfort yourselves together, and edify one another, even as also ye do." They are to comfort or exhort one another on the basis of this truth and also to edify or build up one another in the Christian faith. After a further series of exhortations in I Thessalonians 5:12-22, Paul concludes with the final appeal again stemming from the hope of the Lord's return: "And the very God of peace sanctify you wholly; and I pray God your whole spirit and soul and body be preserved blameless unto the coming of our Lord Jesus Christ." They are, therefore, exhorted, to be living not as those who anticipate a time of dark tribulation such as the great tribulation, nor the Day of the Lord with its hour of the wrath of God poured out upon the earth, but they should be rather looking forward in anticipation and joyous expectation to the coming of the Lord in seeking to live day by day by the power of the Spirit in such a way that they will be preserved blameless in body, soul, and spirit at that future wonderful event. In closing the first epistle, he assures them in I Thessalonians 5:24, "Faithful is he that calleth you, who also will do it."

The glad day when these events will be fulfilled for the Christian may soon be upon us, for if the coming of the Lord was imminent in the first century, it is even more so in this present hour. The promises of God stand undimmed from the erosion of time, and in God's appointed hour He will come for His own even as the infallible Word of God promises.

CHAPTER VI

THE TRANSLATION OF THE CHURCH

Though the translation of the living church is expressly
taught in I Thessalonians 4:17 and implied in numerous
other passages including John 14:3, its formal exposition
was undertaken later by the Apostle Paul in I Corinthians
15:51-58. This passage and I Thessalonians 4:13 – 5:11 are
the two classic passages on the rapture of the church and
constitute its major exposition.

The Context of the Translation in I Corinthians

The revelation concerning the translation of the living church in I Corinthians 15:51-58 comes as the climax
to the divine instruction as found in the preceding chapters.
The Corinthian church had the unenvied distinction of por-
traying in its experience most of the frailties of the church
throughout its history. After only a brief introduction in the
first chapter, the apostle plunged immediately into a long
series of admonitions and rebukes. The Corinthian church
was divided into four parties, those following Paul, Apollos,
Cephas, and Christ. Their differences had arisen from their
adoption of human leaders and those following Christ were
perhaps the most hypocritical. The Corinthians had also
imbibed some of the Greek pride in their heritage, and their
love of worldly wisdom had led them to regard the preaching of the cross as rather naive. Paul had to defend the
Gospel as the wisdom of God. The apostle also rebuked
them for being carnal and unable to receive the deeper
things of divine revelation. He had to chide them for building their lives of wood, hay, and stubble, when they should
have been erecting edifices of gold, silver, and precious
stone, upon the foundation which is Jesus Christ.

In the church at Corinth, there was a notorious case of incest which they had not judged or regarded seriously. In their midst also were those who were going to courts of law to settle their disputes. Some of their number had apparently stumbled at the sanctity of the human body and were at least tempted to return to the gross immorality which characterized the pagan religions of that day. The apostle had to enlarge upon the sanctity of marriage and the responsibility it represents to Christians.

The matter of Christian liberty was also a serious problem in the Corinthian church. Some of their number tended to continue their fellowship with pagans who worshiped idols, and the Corinthians had to be reminded that they would only hurt their testimony by association in the pagan feasts. The church at Corinth had been guilty also of disorders at the Lord's table, observing it in an irreverent and thoughtless manner and without proper spiritual preparation.

Three long chapters had to be devoted to their foolish exaltation of the gift of tongues and the gift of healing, to the neglect of important gifts of proclaiming the Word of God and teaching it faithfully. In the process of all these difficulties, the Corinthian church had lost sight of the fact that service without love is empty. The exhortation of the apostle as contained in I Corinthians 13 is a classic in Biblical exhortation. It was only after this debris had been cleared away that Paul was able to get to the subject that was most on his heart, namely, the great fundamentals of the faith including the precious truths of the Lord's return for His own.

THE DOCTRINE OF RESURRECTION

In the opening verses of the fifteenth chapter of I Corinthians, Paul reminded them of the Gospel that he preached which had resulted in their salvation. He defined this Gospel as the fact that Christ died and rose again, "For I delivered unto you first of all that which I also received, how that Christ died for our sins according to the

scriptures" (I Corinthians 15:3, 4). In affirming the fact
that Christ died for our sins according to the Scriptures,
the apostle is reminding them that this is a fulfillment of
the plan of God foretold early in the Old Testament and
now fulfilled in the work of Christ on Calvary. The fact that
Christ is buried indicates the certainty of His death lest any
should foolishly believe that He merely had swooned and
had not really died.

They are again reminded that Christ rose from the
dead on the third day, according to the Scriptures, allud-
ing to the prophecies of Psalm 16:10, which Peter had also
cited in his Pentecostal sermon in Acts 2:22-31. In the
verses which follow, Paul presents the proofs which demonstrate the certainty of His bodily resurrection, namely that
He was seen of Cephas, then of the Twelve, and on one
occasion by more than five hundred people at once. As far
as the apostle himself was concerned, the final proof was
the appearance of Christ to him on the way to Damascus.

Having established the certainty of the resurrection of
Christ, the argument then proceeds to the theology which
results from this event. Some in the Corinthian church, as
he indicates in I Corinthians 15:12, had denied bodily
resurrection of the dead. The apostle demonstrates that if
Christ is not risen, then there is no Christian faith. The
Gospel also becomes meaningless and Paul's preaching becomes empty. As a matter of fact, the apostle says that
those who preach the Gospel would be "false witnesses of
God" when they preached His death for our sins and His
bodily resurrection if actually there were no bodily resurrection. He concludes in I Corinthians 15:19, "If in this life
only we have hope in Christ, we are of all men most miser-
able."

Having demonstrated the theological necessity of the
resurrection of Christ for the total Christian faith, Paul
builds the whole future program of God upon the fact of
Christ's resurrection, including not only the resurrection
of men but the ultimate victory of Christ over the world

"when he shall have put down all rule and all authority and all power" (I Corinthians 15:24). A long discussion follows, showing the necessity of death and resurrection. The present body of sinful men is not suited for the presence of God due to the fact that it is mortal or subject to death. The human body is natural and belongs to this world and is corruptible or subject to decay and age. What man needs is a spiritual body suited for the presence of God, a body which will not grow old and which will not be subject to death. The normal means for obtaining this body is for the old body to die and to be buried, and the new body must be formed in the act of resurrection as in the case of Jesus Christ. This is God's appointed method of solving the problem stated in I Corinthians 15:50, "that flesh and blood cannot inherit the kingdom of God; neither doth corruption inherit incorruption." It is with this comprehensive introduction that the apostle moves now in the latter part of this chapter into the great truth of the translation of the church.

THE MYSTERY OF THE TRANSLATION OF THE CHURCH

In I Corinthians 15:51-53, the wonderful truth is announced that the bodies of living saints at the time of the coming of the Lord will be instantly transformed from mortal bodies to immortal and from corruptible bodies to incorruptible: "Behold, I shew you a mystery; We shall not all sleep, but we shall all be changed, in a moment, in the twinkling of an eye, at the last trump: for the trumpet shall sound, and the dead shall be raised incorruptible, and we shall be changed. For this corruptible must put on incorruption, and this mortal must put on immortality."

It is most significant that this truth is introduced as "a mystery." The word *mystery* is found twenty-seven times in the New Testament and is used to describe a divine secret not revealed in the Old Testament but revealed at least to some extent in the New. The descriptive definition given in Colossians 1:26 brings this out: "Even the mystery which hath been hid from ages and from generations, but now is made manifest to his saints." The truth of the translation of the church is therefore described as New Testament truth.

The Old Testament records the notable illustration of translation in the cases of Enoch and of Elijah who went to heaven without dying. There is no intimation in the Old Testament of the idea of a whole generation of saints being translated in this way. By contrast, the Old Testament in its prophecies of the second coming of Christ shows life as continuing on earth and the saints surviving the great tribulation are seen entering the millennial earth and continuing in their natural state. It is for this reason that the apostle declares that the truth of the translation of the church is a mystery.

It was, of course, no secret that when Christ would come back to earth to establish His kingdom there would be living people on earth at that time who would be numbered among the saints. This, of course, was anticipated in Old Testament prophecies concerning His second coming, but no rapture is ever indicated in these prophecies. The new truth which is here being revealed relates to an earlier coming of Christ, preceding the tribulation. Saints living on earth at the time of the rapture will never die physically, but instead will experience an instantaneous change from their present bodies to bodies that are suited for the presence of God. This transformation is the translation of the church and parallels the resurrection of the dead in Christ. According to verse 52 it will occur in a moment and in the twinkling of an eye. In other words, it will take place instantaneously at the sounding of the last trump. This trump is to be identified with the trump of God in I Thessalonians 4:16 and is not to be confused with other trumps that deal with other issues such as the trumps of the angels in the book of Revelation or the trump gathering all the elect in Matthew 24:31. The context relates this trump to the resurrection of the dead in Christ and the translation of living saints. It does not have any effect upon the population of the world as a whole and is not related to any judgment such as will be inflicted upon the earth in the end times.

Just as the dead in Christ receive a new body by resurrection, so living saints will be given a new body by translation. Instantaneously, they will exchange the bodies which they have in this present life for new bodies described in this revelation as incorruptible and immortal. They are incorruptible in the sense that they will be ageless and not subject to the normal progression of decay which is so manifest in natural life. They will also be immortal or deathless. Apparently their bodies thus transformed will endure forever. Though the apostle does not state it in so many words, it is obvious also that their bodies will be holy, patterned after the resurrection body of Christ. According to I John 3:2, "When he shall appear, we shall be like him; for we shall see him as he is." Christians living today, therefore, have the prospect of this instantaneous change at the time that the Lord comes back to raise the dead in Christ and to translate the living church.

Aside from the revelation given in I Corinthians 15, there is no other extended passage dealing with the resurrection body and its characteristics. The apostle's description makes clear that the resurrection body will be incorruptible (I Corinthians 15:42), a body of glory (cf. Philippians 3:21), and power (v. 43), a spiritual rather than a natural body (v. 44), a heavenly body (vv. 48, 49), and an immortal body (v. 53).

Much light is cast on the truth of our resurrection body by examining the description of the body of Christ following His resurrection. Prior to the resurrection of Christ, there were numerous cases of people raised from the dead and restored to life. In all these instances, such as that of Lazarus in John 11, the resurrection is in the form of restoration, that is, those restored to life receive the same body which they had when they died. It is assumed that all of these characters in Scripture died subsequently and their bodies were buried. Actually, their resurrection was a restoration, not a transformation such as is expected in the resurrection of Christ. When Christ rose from the dead, He began the order of the first resurrection, mentioned in Revelation 20:5, 6, as including the resurrection of all the saints regardless of time.

At the time of the resurrection of Christ, according to Matthew 27:52, 53, following the earthquake and the rending of the temple, "the graves were opened; and many bodies of the saints which slept arose, and came out of the grave after his resurrection, and went into the holy city, and appeared unto many." This mysterious event attending the resurrection of Christ is nowhere explained in the Bible. A careful reading of the passage will indicate that the resurrection here mentioned took place not at the time of the death of Christ, but after His resurrection as stated in Matthew 27:53. It would hardly seem possible for them to have been raised from the dead and remain in the grave in that state for three days. Therefore, the statement that they came out of the grave after His resurrection also seems to date the time of the resurrection. Though some believe that these were only restored to life, the preferable view is that they actually were raised and given resurrection bodies. There is no evidence that this resurrection included all the saints of the Old Testament, but rather only a few. The passage does not say that all the saints arose but only that "many bodies" were involved.

It is probable that the reason for this strange event stems from the ceremony of the feast of the first fruits which was part of Israel's religious program for each year. In the feast of first fruits as described in Leviticus 23:9-14, the children of Israel were instructed at the time when the harvest began to bring a sheaf of the grain unto the priest. The priest would wave this before the Lord, offering a male lamb as a sacrifice along with a meal offering and a drink offering. The significance of the sheaf of grain was that it was not only one stalk but a handful. The handful was a token of the coming complete harvest. This accordingly was fulfilled at the time of the resurrection of Christ. The great fact was not only that Christ Himself was raised from the dead but that this was the token of the harvest to come. The saints, therefore, who were raised after Christ's resurrection were the divine pledge of God's intent to raise all the saints in their order and according to the divine program.

Of great significance, however, is the series of appearances of Christ following His resurrection. According to John 20, the first appearance was to Mary Magdalene. She had come early in the morning and found the tomb empty and had rushed back to tell the disciples that someone had taken the body of her precious Lord. After delivering her message, she had come back to the garden and there was weeping not knowing what else to do about the situation. As she looked into the sepulchre, she saw two angels, according to John 20:12, who said to her, "Woman, why weepest thou?" (John 20:13). She replied, "Because they have taken away my Lord, and I know not where they have laid Him" (John 20:13). Turning around, she saw Jesus standing but did not recognize Him. Jesus addressed her, "Woman, why weepest thou? whom seekest thou?" (John 20:15). Mary did not immediately recognize the Lord possibly because she was weeping and took Him to be the gardener. In addressing Him accordingly, she said, "Sir, if thou have borne him hence, tell me where thou hast laid him, and I will take him away" (John 20:15). At this query, Jesus replied simply, "Mary."

Recognizing His voice, Mary said, "Rabboni" (John 20:16), or "Master." Jesus then said to her, "Touch me not, for I am not yet ascended to my father: but go to my brethren, and say unto them, I ascend unto my Father, and your Father; and to my God, and your God" (John 20:17). From the fact that Jesus told her "Touch me not," literally, "Stop clinging to me," it seemed that Mary in her ecstasy had embraced her Lord bodily. Christ gently reproved her by reminding her that He had not yet ascended to His Father and instructed her to tell the brethren of His resurrection.

In the details of Mary's encounter with Christ, two important facts stand out. First, Mary recognized Christ's voice. From this preliminary statement, it can be seen that the resurrection body is to be identified with the body of this life in various ways including that of voice. Our loved ones in heaven will not be strangers to us and regardless of what language may be used in heaven, we will be able to recognize their voices as the voices of those whom we loved and held in earth. Second, it is obvious that in embracing the Lord there is a testimony to the reality of the resurrection body. Mary did not grasp thin air. This was not simply a mirage or a spirit. Christ had a real body. This, of course, is a natural deduction from the fact that His body in which He had died on the cross had departed from the tomb. The old body was gone. The new body, though it had differing characteristics, was nevertheless a real body.

Later, when the other women went to meet the Lord according to Matthew 28:9, they were greeted by Christ, "All hail." The passage goes on to say, "And they came and held him by the feet, and worshipped him." Here again it is evident that Christ had a real body and that when they held Him by the feet they found there was real substance to them. In fact, as we learn later, the nailprints were still in the feet from His crucifixion. Still later, on the resurrection day, the Scriptures record that Christ met Peter. There was a wonderful restoration of the one who had denied his Lord thrice (Luke 24:34; I Corinthians 15:5).

The next appearance was to the disciples on the road to Emmaus, recorded in Luke 24:13-32. In this extended passage in which Christ discusses His own death and resurrection with Cleopas and His unnamed companion, He was not immediately known to these disciples. This is explained in Luke 24:16 by the fact that "their eyes were holden that they should not know him." In other words, if there had not been a supernatural blindness imposed upon them, they would have immediately recognized the Lord. Considering the natural unbelief and incredulity attending the recognition of one who has died and has been raised from the dead, it is most significant that in the resurrection appearances the identity of the Lord is unquestioned, and any delay in His recognition is always carefully explained in the Scriptures. In this instance, Christ in order to minister to these disciples withheld His identification until he had unfolded the wonderful truth of the Messianic prophecies of the Old Testament. How marvelous it would have been if we could have had this discussion recorded for us today.

It was not until they came to Emmaus at the eventide and Christ "took bread, and blessed it, and brake, and gave to them," that "their eyes were open, and they knew him" (Luke 24:30, 31). However, as soon as they recognized Him, He vanished from their sight. Then they became aware of the fact that there had been a strange excitement in their hearts as they had talked with Him concerning the Old Testament Scriptures. Luke 24:32 says, "And they said one to another, Did not our heart burn within us, while he talked with us by the way, and while he opened to us the scriptures?" Luke records that they then returned to Jerusalem and found the eleven faithful disciples. From them, the two disciples learned that Christ had indeed been raised from the dead and had appeared to Simon Peter who was there. Then they also gave their report how Christ had appeared to them in the way and how He was revealed to them when He broke the bread.

Having already thus appeared four times on the resurrection day, the fifth appearance is now recorded in Luke 24:36. Apparently without any opening of the door, Christ is revealed to have suddenly appeared in the room. Luke 24:36 states, "And as they thus spake, Jesus himself stood in the midst of them, and saith unto them, Peace be unto you." Such a dramatic appearance, of course, terrified them as recorded in Luke 24:37. They thought they were seeing a spirit. In reply, however, Christ said unto them, "Why are ye troubled? and why do thoughts arise in your hearts? Behold my hands and my feet, that it is I myself: handle me, and see; for a spirit hath not flesh and bones, as ye see me have" (Luke 24:38, 39). From this pronouncement of Christ, a number of things become immediately apparent.

First of all, the disciples had no reason for fear. The fact of the resurrection should be a tremendous comfort and blessing to believers, and Christ wanted His disciples to enter into this glorious truth. In order to dissipate their fear that He was an apparition, He invited them to inspect His hands and His feet. It is evident from John 20:27, in a later appearance, that the nailprints were still in His hands and the wounds still in His side, and it may be presumed that the nailprints were still also in His feet. Here was unmistakable evidence that this was indeed Christ and not someone else. His was a real body to be identified with the one that died on the cross even though marvelously transformed and changed into a resurrection body. He invites them to handle Him, indicating that His body was a body of tangible form.

Further He declares that He has both flesh and bones. From this can be learned that the resurrection body is not a body which deceived the senses and gave the impression of being a physical body without the corresponding reality. Christ says that His body had both flesh and bones. The resurrection body, therefore, will correspond to our present physical bodies in outward characteristics and will have both flesh and bone, though the actual physical substance may differ. It is most significant, however, that no mention is made of blood. In I Corinthians 15:50, Paul had concluded: "Now this I say, brethren, that flesh and blood cannot inherit the kingdom of God; neither doth corruption inherit incorruption." By this, Paul meant the type of flesh that we have now with its blood virculation which sustains the body is not a suitable type of body for heaven. Our resurrection body will have a new flesh which will be sinless and not subject to the restoration principles involved in our present body.

As the disciples pondered these proofs of the resurrection of Christ, for joy they could hardly bring themselves to believe the evidence which was before them (Luke 24: 41). Christ asked them for food (Luke 24:42, 43), and taking the broiled fish and honey, He ate it before them. It was another form of demonstration that He had a real body and was not merely a spirit. It also introduced the interesting conclusion that in their resurrection bodies, the saints will be able to eat food, though apparently it will not be necessary for sustaining life or strength.

Though Luke 24:33 indicates that the disciples returning from Emmaus had gone to the "eleven gathered together," it is evident from John 20:24 that Thomas was not there and only ten of the eleven disciples were actually in the upper room. It was not until a week later that Thomas had the joy of meeting his Lord. The subsequent experience, however, confirms the evidence previously presented. Thomas, according to John 20:25, found it impossible to believe that Jesus was actually raised from the dead and had said to the disciples: "Except I shall see in his hands the print of the nails, put my finger into the print of the nails, and thrust my hand into his side, I will not believe."

A week later, as Thomas and the other disciples were in a room with the door shut, Jesus again appeared to them and, as in His former appearance, said, "Peace be unto you" (John 20:26). Then addressing Himself to Thomas, our Lord said, "Reach hither thy finger, and behold my hands; and reach hither thy hand, and thrust it into my side: and be not faithless, but believing" (John 20:27). In reply, Thomas, forgetting his unbelief and his dogmatic demands for factual evidence replied, "My Lord and my God" (John 20:28). Thomas needed no proof. The evidence was all too clear that this was indeed the Lord and Saviour.

The fact, however, that Christ invited him to inspect His body to see the evidences of His crucifixion proves that it was the same body which died on the cross. In commenting on Thomas' unbelief changed into faith, Christ said, "Thomas, because thou hast seen me, thou hast believed: blessed are they that have not seen, and yet have believed" (John 20:29).

Subsequent appearances of Christ confirm this evidence. The body of Christ was identified with the body He had prior to His death. It was a body of flesh and bone which had real substance. His voice as well as His general appearance could be identified as belonging to the same person who was with the disciples through their years of fellowship with Him prior to Calvary. It was a body, therefore, which could be seen and felt, a body which could consume food, a body which in many respects corresponds in appearance to our present earthly bodies, and yet marvelously delivered from limitations which hinder here. There is no evidence, for instance, that Christ walked back from Emmaus to Jerusalem. Apparently transportation takes on a new character for a resurrection body. It was also true that He could enter rooms with the doors being shut, indicating that physical confinement is not possible for a resurrection body. In all of these things, the testimony is that the resurrection body of believers, patterned after the resurrection body of Christ, will be wonderfully delivered from the limitations of this life and will be gloriously suited for the immediate presence of the Lord.

A most significant fact is often overlooked in I Corinthians 15:51-53 in that the passage states plainly, "We shall all be changed." In the consideration of the problem of the time of the rapture, many have followed the conclusion that the translation of the church is somehow to be identified as a part of Christ's coming to establish His kingdom on the earth. This is known as the post-tribulation rapture view as opposed to the pretribulation rapture teaching which holds that the translation takes place some years before Christ returns to establish His kingdom. In the simple expression, "We shall all be changed," there seems to be decisive evidence that the rapture must be distinguished from the second coming of Christ to the earth. In fact, it demands that there be a considerable time period between these two events.

If an attempt is made to reconstruct the usual post-tribulational concept, it is evident that in order to accommodate I Thessalonians 4:17 the rapture must take place in the process of Christ's procession from heaven to the earth at that moment when He enters the atmospheric heaven. In other words, the rapture in the post-tribulation theory must occur before Christ ever actually comes to the earth itself and His feet touch the Mount of Olives (Zechariah 14:4). It should be further evident that, if the rapture takes place at this time, all the saints will be with the Lord in the air and all the remaining people on the earth are those who are not saved.

The Scriptures seem to indicate plainly that at the second coming of Christ all unbelievers are purged out. This is the teaching of the parable of the wheat and the tares, and it is plainly indicated in such passages as Revelation 14:9-12 which reveals that all worshipers of the beast will be put to death. According to Revelation 13:8, everyone on earth will worship the beast except true believers. According to Matthew 25:31-46, the goats representing the unsaved among Gentiles will also be purged out as will the rebels of Israel representing unbelief in Israel according to Ezekiel 20:38.

Those who hold the premillennial interpretation of Scripture are, therefore, faced with an insuperable problem if they attempt to accommodate this with the post-tribulational idea. If all the wicked are put to death and if all the saints are translated, it leaves no one in their natural bodies to populate the millennial earth. Hence, the simple fact that everyone will be transformed who believes in Christ on the occasion of the rapture of the church makes it necessary to move this event forward and leave a sufficient time period between the rapture and Christ's coming

to establish His kingdom to raise up a whole new generation of saints from both Jews and Gentiles to populate the
millennial earth. Thus, the godly remnant of Israel will
come into being after the rapture and during the time of
trouble preceding the second coming of Christ. Likewise
among the Gentiles there will be raised up a host of believers, some of whom will survive the martyrdom, which
many will suffer, and will be on earth waiting for the coming of the Lord. These will be the sheep of Matthew 25.
There seems to be built into the revelation concerning
the rapture of the church that this is an event distinct from
the second coming and one which could not be fulfilled si-
multaneously with it.

The expression, "We shall all be changed," is also significant as making impossible the contention of those who
hold to a partial rapture, namely, that at the coming of
Christ for His church only those especially spiritual or un-
usually well prepared who are looking for His coming will
be raptured. It is rather that "all" will be involved. This
means all Christians in Christ, whether they are what they
ought to be or not, are raised from the dead, if in the grave,
or translated, if living in the earth. The issue will not be
spirituality but whether they have been born again and
have been baptized into the body of Christ by the Spirit
of God.

A careful study of the major rapture narratives found in
I Corinthians 15 and I Thessalonians 4 would do much to
correct the confusion that exists in the modern church
concerning the time and character of the rapture itself.
Too often theories are advanced with little reference to
the details of these specific revelations, and with an impa-
tience to account for the specifics which are enfolded in
the Word of God.

As previously indicated, "the last trump" is to be
identified with the trump of I Thessalonians 4:16 where it
is called "the trump of God." The question, however, has
been raised why the words, "the last," should be used. It
seems apparent from Matthew 24:31 that this is not the last

trumpet in the sequence of events. The answer seems to be simply that this is the final call for the church. Whether or not there are any previous trumpets to be sounded in the history of the church, this is the last one. As pointed out earlier, it may be that Paul is using a familiar pattern established in his day by the Roman soldiers. As was commonly known, a series of trumpets marked the beginning of their day; the first, raising them from sleep, the second, calling them to form the march of the day, and the third or last in the series, signaling the beginning of the march. The last trump then is for the church a "forward march" or actually a command to rise to meet the Lord in the air. The church previously had heard the call of the Gospel through the convicting power of the Spirit. They had listened to the exhortation of the Word of God as applied by the Spirit to their life and witness. Now the time had come to begin the majestic march to glory and the last trump sounded. If normal rules of exegesis be applied to this, the passage loses much of its problem. The context plainly indicates that this trump has to do with resurrection and translation whereas other trumps of the New Testament have an entirely different context and in none of them is either resurrection or translation involved.

THE HOPE OF VICTORY OVER DEATH

In I Corinthians 15:54-57, the apostle sounds a note of praise for the victory over death which Christians translated at the rapture will experience. This will be shared by those who have died and are raised from the dead at this time. He writes the Corinthians, "So when this corruptible shall have put on incorruption, and this mortal shall have put on immortality, then shall be brought to pass the saying that is written, Death is swallowed up in victory. O death, where is thy sting? O grave, where is thy victory? The sting of death is sin; and the strength of sin is the law. But thanks be to God, which giveth us the victory through our Lord Jesus Christ" (I Corinthians 15:54-57).

The ultimate victory for all Christians will be achieved on that glad day when corruption and mortality will be replaced by incorruption and immortality. Paul says that then will be fulfilled the prediction of Isaiah 25:8 embodied in the expression, "Death is swallowed up in victory." It should be obvious that the translation and resurrection of the church is only a partial fulfillment of the Isaiah passage, as Isaiah contemplates this as it embraces all humanity including Israel. The final victory over death does not come until after the millennium. At present, Christians do not have victory over death, but when this event takes place their victory will be complete and no longer will they be subject to death and decay.

As the apostle exults in the coming victory over death, he raises the question, "O death, where is thy sting? O grave, where is thy victory?" (I Corinthians 15:55). He gives the answer in verse 56, "The sting of death is sin, and the strength of sin is the law." Physical death afflicts the Christian because of the inexorable law of judgment pronounced upon Adam that his body should return to the dust. Though Christians are relieved from the guilt of sins, somehow the principle of death continues for those who have died preceding the rapture of the church. That the law is reversed for those translated at the rapture proceeds from the pure grace of God which has satisfied the law and in this case finds it unnecessary to exact this form of divine judgment upon sin. As the apostle states in I Corinthians 15:57, "But thanks be to God, which giveth us the victory through our Lord Jesus Christ." The translation of living saints as well as the resurrection of the dead in Christ is a part of God's program of salvation for those who have put their faith in Christ. It is the ultimate form of salvation which was begun at the moment of faith in Christ and completes the plan of God that every true believer should be presented faultless in His presence. By faith, the Christian even in the midst of earth's trials can contemplate this future victory which will be true of every Christian, made possible entirely by the finished work of

Christ on the cross and His own triumph over death in bodily resurrection.

As in other prophetic portions of the New Testament, the truth of the rapture leads naturally to a stirring exhortation with which chapter fifteen of I Corinthians concludes, "Therefore, my beloved brethren, be ye stedfast, unmoveable, always abounding in the work of the Lord, forasmuch as ye know that your labour is not in vain in the Lord." Here is the watchword for those who are looking for the coming of the Lord. They should first of all be steadfast, a word meaning to become seated or to put your full weight upon. God wants us to rest upon these promises and depend upon the certain fulfillment of the promises of resurrection and translation. In facing the storms of life, the Christian should also be unmoveable. This solid situation can only be possible as the Christian rests upon Christ the Rock who cannot be moved. The exhortation, however, does not contemplate simply standing or holding our ground, but the idea is presented that if we believe in the coming of the Lord, we should be "always abounding in the work of the Lord." This superabundant expression indicates that Christians should be busy about our Lord's work at all times and to the greatest possible extent. The teaching of the rapture does not properly lead to an attitude of the folded hands. There is much to be done and the time is short. One who believes the rapture will instead be ceaselessly active in the work while there is yet time.

The apostle concludes the exhortation by the reminder, "Forasmuch as ye know that your labour is not in vain in the Lord." Following the rapture of the church will come the judgment seat of Christ when the church in heaven receives her rewards. Christians are reminded that there is a day of reckoning coming when they as stewards must give an account. It will be a glad day for those who have been faithful in their service for the Lord as they receive their just due.

CHAPTER VII

THE IMPORTANCE OF THE RAPTURE

The doctrine of the coming of the Lord for His own with its promise of the resurrection of the dead in Christ and the translation of the living church was a prominent feature in the church of the first century. Most scholars agree that the early church believed in the imminent return of the Lord and considered it a possibility that the Lord could come at any time. Such a hope seemed to have permeated apostolic thinking. In I and II Thessalonians, for instance, it is mentioned in every chapter. Most of the epistles make some mention of the coming of the Lord and anticipate the end of the age.

In spite of the apostolic emphasis on the doctrine, there is a studied avoidance of the subject in much of the theological literature of the past and present. Many systematic theologies barely mention the subject of the rapture, and, if mentioned at all, it is included as a minor phase of end-time events. In modern liberalism and neo-orthodoxy, no attention whatever is paid to the subject of the rapture. Even in conservative theological discussion, the tendency is to play down the importance of this theme of Scripture.

This neglect of the doctrine of the rapture is all the more remarkable because the place given to the rapture in any system of theology is a significant commentary upon its theological premises, its hermeneutical principles, and its prophetic program as a whole. An analysis of the doctrine of the rapture in relationship to theology as a whole will demonstrate that the doctrine has significance far beyond its own particulars, and that, therefore, conclusions reached concerning the rapture reveal a system of thought. The contention of some contemporary scholars that eschatology is unimportant and that the rapture doctrine in particular is a matter of little interest to theology as a whole is an error of considerable proportion.

THEOLOGICAL PREMISES OF THE RAPTURE

In the study of the truth concerning the rapture of the church, it soon becomes apparent that one of the major issues is the inspiration of the Scriptures. Modern liberals who deny that the Bible is the infallible Word of God have in general taken the position that prophecy is an impossibility. Passages in the New Testament, therefore, which speak of the rapture they consider a record of the hope of the early church or in some cases a statement of divine purpose. They do not believe that prophecy should be accepted at face value as a bona fide prediction of a future event. Liberals, when pressed, will acknowledge that human life cannot go on forever and that there must be some end to human existence in this present state. Nevertheless, they deny that the Bible outlines in any specific way a future program which will be literally fulfilled. The disinterest of the church at large in the doctrine of the rapture may be traced in part to this attitude of unbelief in prophecy as a whole and questions concerning the authority, integrity, and accuracy of Scripture. Accordingly, writers who do not accept the infallibility of the Scriptures seldom add anything to the doctrine of the rapture, and for the most part avoid or ignore the subject completely.

Only theological conservatives can engage in any vital discussion concerning the rapture. Normally, they hold to the concept that the Bible can predict the future. Regardless of their particular point of view, they usually agree that the Bible predicts the end of the age and a personal, bodily return of the Lord. For such, the question is how the passages dealing with the translation of the living church and the resurrection of the dead in Christ relate to end-time events. Their judgments in these areas are largely determined by their broader eschatological conviction, namely, whether they are premillennial, postmillennial, or amillennial.

Generally speaking, amillenarians, such as have followed the traditional view of Augustine, have combined the doctrine of the rapture with the second coming of Christ to the earth at the end of the age. They seldom, therefore, give separate consideration to this truth and regard it merely as an incident in the total program which brings human history to a close. One, therefore, can hardly expect an amillenarian to deal adequately with this doctrine. Usually their writings tend to refute pretribulationism or premillennialism, as the case might be, rather than to set up their own doctrine of the rapture.

Practically the same point of view is adopted by the postmillennialist of the conservative type. They, too, tend to combine all end-time events as having their culmination in the second coming of Christ, and the rapture becomes a phase of this program. In their writings likewise the rapture is given scant attention. It is only in premillennial discussion that the rapture doctrine has assumed any large proportion. For all practical purposes, a formal consideration of the rapture of the church, including the debate as to when it will occur in relationship to other events, is a problem within premillennialism.

If the view of the partial rapture concept be excluded, there are three major viewpoints advocated today, namely, pretribulationism, midtribulationism, and post-tribulationism. Of primary interest and contrast is the post-tribulational view as compared to the pretribulational view. Post-tribulationism views the rapture as occurring in the sequence of events described as the second coming of Christ. They believe the church will be raptured at the time Christ is descending from heaven to the earth. The church will be translated, according to I Thessalonians 4, meet the Lord in the air, and then continue with the heavenly throng to. the earth to accompany Christ in His establishment of the millennial kingdom. The post-tribulational view, as held by some premillenarians, is often quite similar to that advocated by the amillenarian, differing from it principally in its concept of the millennial reign of Christ following the rapture. For the amillenarian the eternal age begins immediately.

The post-tribulationism of our day in some respects corresponds to the view of the early church fathers and in other aspects is decidedly different and recent. In the church of the second and third century, it was commonly believed that the church was already in the great tribulation predicted by Christ. For this reason, they believed in the imminency of Christ's return as an event which could happen any day. Their view of the Lord's return was that it was both post-tribulational and imminent.

Most conservative scholarship agrees that the early church fathers were in error in their conclusion that they were already in the great tribulation. The passing of the centuries makes it clear that their persecutions were those which could be normally expected throughout the age rather than the particular trials which could be expected in the great tribulation. Modern post-tribulationists, however, believe that the early church fathers were right in their conclusion concerning post-tribulationism even if they were wrong in believing they were already in the great tribulation. In contrast to the early fathers, however, modern post-tribulationists do not believe in imminency in the same sense as did the early church, but rather hold that certain events must take place first, namely, the events outlined in the Scriptures as preceding the second coming of Christ to the earth. Modern post-tribulationists, therefore, while affirming post-tribulationism as such, deny imminency in the sense of an any-moment return, and hold a decidedly different point of view from the early church fathers.

In contrast to post-tribulationism, the pretribulational position holds that the rapture of the church is an event separated from the second coming of Christ to the earth by a period of time usually considered to be at least seven years on the basis of Daniel's prophecies in Daniel 9:27. Pretribulationists therefore generally accept the doctrine of imminency, that is, that Christ could come at any moment. They deny post-tribulationism, and hold that there must be a period of time between the rapture and the second coming itself during which certain events of the end time must be fulfilled. Since these events are viewed as following rather than preceding the rapture, there is nothing hindering the rapture occurring any day.

A third view largely promoted in our present generation is the so-called midtribulational view which places the rapture three and one-half years before Christ's second coming to establish His kingdom. There is comparatively no literature on the subject and few scholars have been willing to advocate openly this point of view. Some have adopted it, apparently motivated primarily by the desire to mediate the pretribulational and post-tribulational view and accept some tenets from both views. Though this interpretation has proved attractive to some, it has not as yet assumed any large proportion in the scholarship and writings related to the rapture doctrine. While it has certain advantages over both pretribulationism and post-tribulationism, it creates problems which are far greater than the benefits derived. While the midtribulational view would lend itself to some extent to a considerable treatment of the doctrine of the rapture as a separate aspect of the Christian hope, from a practical standpoint it has not done so and writers who have contributed in this area have done little to enhance the doctrine of the rapture as a whole.

In comparing the theological premises of the various views of the rapture, it soon becomes apparent that those who observe some dispensational distinction tend to the pretribulational rapture position whereas those who hold to covenant theology or kingdom theology tend toward the midtribulational or post-tribulational position. It is not too much to say that the theological presuppositions which enter into the study of the rapture are usually largely determinative in its outcome. Those who distinguish the program of Israel from the program of the church tend to pretribulationism whereas those who merge the two consider them phases of the soteriological program of God and tend toward midtribulationism or post-tribulationism. One's view on the rapture therefore, becomes indicative of one's theology as a whole, which lends support to the contention that the rapture doctrine is, after all, important theologically.

HERMENEUTICAL PRINCIPLES OF THE RAPTURE

It is gradually being recognized in contemporary theology that hermeneutical principles have much to do with the total problem of establishing eschatology. Amillenarians and premillenarians agree that their respective points of view stem from their principles of interpretation. Augustine, who advanced the dual hermeneutics, has largely set the pattern for amillennial eschatology. He held that while the Scriptures as a whole should be interpreted normally, historically, and grammatically, prophecy was a special case which required spiritualization or allegorical interpretation, and therefore a nonliteral interpretation of prophecy. By contrast, premillenarians generally have adopted a single hermeneutic, namely, that prophecy should be interpreted by the same principles by which any other type of Scripture is interpreted. While some premillenarians, especially those who are not dispensational, have used to some extent the dual hermeneutics of Augustine, the principle still holds that the hermeneutic rather than the individual argument determines the outcome of the discussion.

What is true of premillennialism in contrast to amillennialism is also true of the pretribulational view in contrast to midtribulationism and post-tribulationism. It is impossible to hold the modern point of view of post-tribulationism or midtribulationism without introducing to a considerable degree the principles of spiritualization of prophecy. The specifics of the great tribulation are often ignored. Even within premillennialism, Israel and the church are not kept distinct as to their divine programs. Though a widespread variation exists in the interpretation of end-time events, the tendency has been for post-tribulationism to spiritualize the tribulation whereas pretribulationism tends to take it more literally. A conclusion, therefore, can be fairly reached that in so far as one's hermeneutics follows the pattern of amillennialism, one tends to be post-tribulational and, to the extent that he follows dispensational or literal interpretation, he tends to the pretribulational position. The doctrine of the rapture, therefore, becomes indicative not only of theology as a whole but of the hermeneutics by which its doctrine is established.

Prophetic Program

Not only is the doctrine of the rapture related to the theological premises and hermeneutical principles of a given theology, but a direct relationship can be established between the doctrine of the rapture and the prominence given prophecy as a whole. Generally speaking, amillenarians and postmillenarians do not provide a large place in their systems for prophecy. One never hears of a prophecy conference sponsored by amillenarians or postmillenarians. Such an emphasis on prophecy is almost limited to the premillenarian group. Further, the same distinction can be observed between those who are post-tribulational and midtribulational, as opposed to the pretribulational position. Rarely, if ever, are prophecy conferences conducted by post-tribulationists or midtribulationists even if they are premillennial. It is almost a foregone conclusion that if a church or an institution of learning sponsors a special series of studies in prophecy it is motivated primarily by its pretribulational convictions. The prominence given to prophecy as a whole, therefore, is linked to the prominence given the doctrine of the rapture and vice versa.

Not only is there a link between emphasis on the rapture and emphasis on prophecy as a whole, but the same principle can also be observed in the practical application

of prophecy to the Christian life. While all conservative
points of view share to some extent the blessings of Christian hope such as our ultimate resurrection from the dead
and the blessings which will be experienced by the saints
in heaven, the practical application of prophecy to the daily
life is given additional incentive under the pretribulational
position. This is an obvious deduction from its intrinsic
character.

The fact that Christ could come any day is certainly
more arresting and dramatic than the possibility of His
coming some years hence. The doctrine of imminency is
inevitably related to the pointed application of certain
prophecies. While even a post-tribulationist can claim that
the hope of the coming of the Lord is a purifying hope,
a blessed hope, and a comforting hope, it is nevertheless
true that in proportion as the realization of the hope is imminent so there is increased pertinence to the application.
Hence, in John 14 where Christ tells His disciples, "Let not
your heart be troubled," one of the reasons which He gives
is, "I will come again and receive you unto myself." In a
similar way in the Thessalonian church after outlining to
them the fact that the dead in Christ will be raised just a
moment before the living church is translated, Paul concludes, "Wherefore comfort one another with these words."
The comfort of the possibility of reunion with their loved
ones any day is certainly more pointed and more helpful
than the ultimate possibility of such an event in the distant future.

Of particular relevance is the purifying effect of the
doctrine of the rapture. As mentioned in I John 3:3 and in the
preceding verse, Christians are assured, "When he shall
appear, we shall be like him; for we shall see him as he
is." Then the application is made, "And every man that
hath this hope in him purifieth himself, even as he is pure."
While the hope of being like the Saviour is an incentive to
purity of life regardless of when it occurs, if the event of
the Lord's return could happen at any moment, in any day,

there is an urgency about the whole matter of sanctification in that one wants his life to be in order at the time that the Lord comes. Any housewife can testify to the difference in preparation for an expected guest depending on the expected time of arrival. If she receives a letter stating that some friend plans to visit several years hence, such a letter produces no change in the schedule of the household. If, however, a letter should come saying a guest may be expected any day, this requires an entirely different form of preparation. Ordinary schedules are cancelled in favor of a program of immediate preparedness.

It may be concluded, therefore, that from a practical standpoint, the concept of the rapture held in any system of theology has an important bearing upon its theology as a whole, not so much from the standpoint of being causal, but from the standpoint of being indicative of the theological premises and principles of interpretation of which the doctrine of the rapture is an eloquent expression.

THE RAPTURE IN RELATION TO ORTHODOXY

One of the side effects of a proper emphasis on the doctrine of the rapture is that it seems to have the curious result of promoting orthodoxy in theology as a whole. It is, of course, true that systems of theology which are basically conservative and support the great fundamentals of the faith do not necessarily emphasize the doctrine of the rapture. Failure to agree on the doctrine of the rapture is not per se a token of unorthodoxy in major doctrine.

It is, however, strangely true that in the mainstream of evangelicalism, those who emphasize the imminency of the Lord's return are almost invariably orthodox in the major tenets of their theology. They almost always hold to the verbal and plenary inspiration of the Bible. They inevitably accept the deity of Jesus Christ and the sufficiency of His sacrifice. They have few problems in accepting the miraculous and the accuracy of Scripture as a whole. There is no tendency toward a superficial intellectualism or a philosophical approach to the Bible which robs it of its content and spiritual vigor. While much of modern scholarship writes off any emphasis on the doctrine of the rapture as somewhat naive, it is also significant that such modern scholarship as a whole has not been able to maintain its own orthodoxy. The freshness of the hope of the Lord's return and the day-by-day expectation of the fulfillment of the precious promises relating to the hope of the Christian are a wonderful means of strength for Christians who are tested in their faith. In too many cases where the precious hope of the rapture has become dim, it is the prelude for departure from the faith in the fundamentals, as neglect or unbelief in one area of theology often spreads to another.

Those who adhere strictly to the pretribulational view of the Lord's return should exercise, on the one hand, caution lest they label those who differ from them as heterodox because of failure to agree on this aspect of God's prophetic program. On the other hand, they should not be discouraged by the fact that they are a minority in the total professing church of our day and should stand resolutely for their convictions even if subjected to ridicule and misrepresentation. The precious hope of the Lord's return is far more rewarding than any of its substitutes and though it may not appeal to the intellectuals of our day and may be lacking in sophistication and philosophic ramification and terminology, it nevertheless is deeply satisfying to the devout soul who is looking for the return of His precious Lord any day.

CHAPTER VIII

THE CHURCH AND THE TRIBULATION

One of the important problems in prophecy concerning the church is the relationship of the church to the time of tribulation preceding the second coming of Christ to the earth. Those who approach the subject of prophecy from the viewpoint of the amillennial or postmillennial theology, generally speaking, consider the church as going through this time of trouble with the hope of being translated at the close of the tribulation when Christ comes to earth. Both the resurrection of the dead in Christ and the translation of the living church, therefore, become events immediately preceding the inauguration of the final judgments and the eternal state. Both the postmillennial and amillennial views regard the millennium as already past.

It is only within the premillennial interpretation of prophecy that much attention has been paid to the rapture. A few have followed the partial rapture concept, holding that a portion of the church will be raptured before the tribulation with the rest of the church awaiting rapture at the close of the tribulation. This view, however, has not gained much acceptance and is for practical purposes an oddity rather than a principal consideration in the study of prophecy.

Another view which has attracted a few adherents is the midtribulational view which considers the rapture as taking place three and one-half years before the second coming of Christ to the earth and therefore before what Christ calls "the great tribulation" (Matthew 24:21). They place the rapture at the end of the first half of Daniel's

seventieth week (Daniel 9:27). Relatively few have adopted
this hypothesis. The great majority of premillenarians are
divided between the post-tribulational concept of the rapture and the pretribulational concept. Most contemporary
premillenarians follow the pretribulational view that Christ's
coming for His church precedes the fulfillment of Daniel's
seventieth week, and is therefore before the end-time period of trouble.

The argument for and against these various viewpoints
are detailed in the writer's previously published work *The
Rapture Question* and his *The Millennial Kingdom* as well
as in a host of other publications by many authors. The
more important considerations and a review of the principal
arguments for and against the pretribulational rapture
can be restated here. For the purpose of this discussion,
the midtribulational theory and the partial rapture view,
held only by a small minority, will be disregarded in favor
of a comparison of the post-tribulational and pretribulational points of view.

POST-TRIBULATIONAL INTERPRETATION OF THE RAPTURE

As in the case of other problems of interpretation in the
realm of prophecy, post-tribulationism is determined largely
by the premises which it assumes. Among these premises
is the spiritualization of some of the prophecies pertaining
to the tribulation. Just as the amillenarians and postmillenarians spiritualize the doctrine of the millennium, so post-
tribulationists tend to spiritualize the details of the tribulation. A great variety of opinion, however, exists within the
post-tribulational view. Some contend that the tribulation
itself is not a specific period of time and that it is proper to
consider the church as always being in tribulation. Some
begin the time of tribulation with Adam. Some begin it
with Christ. This post-tribulational explanation regards as
obvious that the church will go through the tribulation because they hold the church is already in the tribulation.

This type of post-tribulationism, of course, disregards
the specific details given in the Word of God concerning the

tribulation such as are found in Jeremiah 30:3-11, Matthew 24:15-30, and extended portions of the book of Revelation. These passages make clear that the great tribulation can only take place after a large portion of Israel has been re-gathered, something that did not occur until the twentieth century. More particularly, it follows the breaking of the covenant made with Israel (Daniel 9:27) when their holy place will be desecrated (Matthew 24:15). No literal fulfillment of this has occurred. If the great tribulation be interpreted literally, it is a three and one-half year period culminating in Christ's second coming to the earth and preceded by a period of three and one-half years during which the covenant made with Israel is observed. Post-tribulationists, therefore, who spiritualize the tribulation by finding supposed fulfillment in the past are following the same principles of interpretation found in amillennialism. It is quite inconsistent to follow an amillennial interpretation of the tribulation and join this to a premillennial interpretation of a millennium.

Other post-tribulationists, however, regard the seventieth week of Daniel as yet future much as do the pretribulationists, but expect the church to be safely conducted through it. This view, while granting to the tribulation a future status, usually involves a severe toning down of the specifics of the judgments poured out on the earth in the tribulation. It is rare to find a post-tribulationist who takes at face value the tremendous judgments portrayed in the book of Revelation. Almost invariably, however, post-tribulationists spiritualize other aspects of prophecy. In particular, they usually consider the church of the present dispensation and the nation Israel as the same body, that is, they regard the church as the true Israel. This is a common teaching of covenant theology and is quite a normal feature of amillennialism. Premillenarians who follow covenant theology usually are post-tribulationists.

Still another approach to the problem is taken by some post-tribulationists who attempt to steer a middle course between spiritualization of the tribulation itself and spiritualization of Israel. Such scholars usually find their unifying principle in the concept of the kingdom and view Israel, the church, and the saints of all ages, as embodied in the kingdom of God. Under this point of view, the church loses its distinctive New Testament character and for all practical purposes is one and the same as the saints of the tribulation time. Such writers find evidence of the church in the tribulation simply from the fact that there are saints in this period. A survey of post-tribulationism therefore demonstrates that it always involves a spiritualization of some entities which pretribulationists consider in a more literal way. Post-tribulationists spiritualize either the tribulation itself, the church and Israel, or follow a soteriological approach to the divine purpose which merges the saints of all ages into one entity.

Post-tribulationism, building upon these premises, attempts to prove that the church is or will be in the tribulation period, and therefore must pass through this time of trial before the rapture itself can occur. A detailed study of post-tribulationism is provided by the writer's discussion in *The Rapture Question*, pp. 127-70.

Most important, however, to the solution of this problem is the fact that post-tribulationists have never proved that the church, the body of Christ, is in the tribulation. On this point, the Scriptures are silent. While post-tribulationists characteristically throw the burden of proof on the pretribulationists and often challenge them to prove that the church is not in the tribulation, it would seem, however, a reasonable point of view to require the post-tribulationists to offer proof. None of the terms relating to the church as the body of Christ in this present age are ever used in relation to tribulation saints. In fact, they are uniformly referred to as either belonging to Israel or to the Gentiles, never as forming the one body described as the church. As the arguments of post-tribulationists are largely of a negative character, namely, an argument against the pretribulational position, the approach which brings the points of issue immediately to the front are the arguments for pretribulationism.

INTERPRETATIVE PRINCIPLES OF PRETRIBULATIONISM

Just as a principle of spiritualization of important concepts in relation to the tribulation is the interpretative approach of post-tribulationism, so the interpretation of prophecy in its normal and literal sense is the key to pretribulationism. Augustine, the father of orthodox amillennialism, adopted a dual hermeneutics which provided for the spiritualization of prophecy though he considered it proper for the rest of Scripture to be interpreted normally and literally. This principle led to the abandonment of premillennialism by the Roman Church. The same principle in smaller dimensions is found in the arguments relating to pretribulationism and post-tribulationism, with the post-tribulationist following a dual hermeneutics like that of Augustine and pretribulationists following a single hermeneutic such as is characteristic of premillennialism.

The literal interpretation of prophecy leads to the conclusion that there is a future time of trouble which will be a major feature of the end time. Daniel's prophecy of a period of seven years culminating Israel's history (Daniel 9:27) is regarded as future and providing the major structure of the period between the rapture and the second coming of Christ. Likewise, the literal interpretation of prophecy maintains a contrast between Israel and the church. The church is a separate body of believers, distinct in the divine purpose of God's plan from the nation Israel and more particularly to be contrasted to His plan for the saved or elect in Israel. The teaching contrasting Israel and the church is sometimes referred to as the dispensational interpretation. Actually, however, the distinction between Israel and the church does not stem from dispensationalism itself, but from the single hermeneutic or the literal interpretation of prophecy. Dispensationalism is the result not the cause of this doctrine.

Pretribulationism also considers the tribulation itself with a large degree of literalness and views the judgments poured out upon the earth revealed in the book of Revelation as subject to literal fulfillment. While recognizing that some of these prophecies are given in symbolic form, the stark awfulness of the future period of tribulation nevertheless emerges from any reasonably literal interpretation of prophecies having to do with the great tribulation. Christ Himself declared that there would be no other time in all of human history equal to that of the great tribulation in severity (Matthew 24:21) and with this agree the prophecies of Jeremiah 30:7, "That none is like it: it is even the time of Jacob's trouble," and the prophecy of Daniel 12:1, "There shall be a time of trouble, such as never was since there was a nation." Undoubtedly the application of literal interpretation to prophecy leads to the pretribulational view whereas the spiritualization of prophecy leads to the post-tribulational view. It is not too much to say that this really determines the issue and that subsequent arguments merely confirm the reasonableness of their respective points of view.

THE HISTORY OF THE PRETRIBULATIONAL INTERPRETATION

Undoubtedly, one of the most impressive arguments used by post-tribulationists is the contention that they represent the view of the early church in contrast to pretribulationism which is new and novel and therefore wrong. The fact is, however, that neither post-tribulationism nor pretribulationism as it is held today corresponds to the viewpoint of the early church fathers. In the early church, the Lord's coming was viewed as imminent, that is, an event which could occur any day. Coupled with the doctrine of imminency, however, was the view that the church was already in the great tribulation and that therefore Christ would come at the close of the time of trouble. The early church did not, therefore, distinguish the rapture from the second coming. It is obvious that this to some extent corresponds to post-tribulationism. However, modern post-tribulationism does not accept the doctrine of imminency, that is, that Christ could come at any moment, and usually regards the future as involving a number of prophecies being fulfilled first, such as that of the great tribulation before Christ could come. Modern post-tribulationism, therefore, generally denies imminency but affirms post-tribulationism in contrast to pretribulationism which denies a post-tribulational rapture but like the early fathers affirms the imminency of the Lord's return.

The truth is that in the study of eschatology there has been considerable progress. Probably more refinement and study has been given to the subject of the future of the church in the last century than for many centuries preceding. There is some evidence that the church has been progressing throughout the centuries of its history through the major areas of doctrine beginning with bibliology and theology proper as in the early centuries of the church, advancing to such subjects as anthropology and hamartiology in the fourth and succeeding centuries, and dealing with soteriology and ecclesiology in the Protestant Reformation. It has been mostly in the last century that eschatology has really come to the fore as an area for scholarly study and debate. It is only natural that there should be refinement and improvement in this area just as there have been in other areas throughout the history of the church.

The fact, therefore, that ideas relating to prophecy are new or sharper in their distinctions than in previous generations is not an argument in itself that the truth thus presented is actually an error. It is evident from the study of such works as Ladd's *The Blessed Hope* and Alexander Reese's *The Approaching Advent* of Christ that the deciding point in their systems was not their exegesis of the Scriptures, but the fact that the early church fathers did not teach pretribulationism as it is now held by its adherents.

The truth is, however, that the early fathers did not hold to post-tribulationism as taught by Ladd and Reese either. The history of the doctrine of the rapture does not really support either post-tribulationism or pretribulationism as it is now held. The ultimate question, after all, is not what the fathers taught but what the Bible teaches. In their understanding of prophecy as in many other areas, the early church fathers were immature and perhaps have been given a halo of orthodoxy which they only partially deserved. Pretribulationists can point to the early church fathers as being chiliastic or premillennial and as believers in the imminent return of Christ. They cannot, however, claim that the specifies of their view were held by the early church any more than most post-tribulationists can do so with complete accuracy.

The Pretribulational Concept of the Tribulation

Though some variation exists in pretribulational teaching about the tribulation, in general pretribulationists hold that there will be a period of at least seven years between the rapture of the church and Christ's coming to establish His kingdom in the earth. Many pretribulationists believe that immediately after the rapture there will be a short period of preparation. During this period the revived Roman Empire will come into being, formed of ten nations as predicted in Daniel 7 and Revelation 13. The one who becomes the head of this ten-nation confederacy is identified as "the prince that shall come" of Daniel 9:26 who according to Daniel 9:27 makes a covenant of seven years duration with the people of Israel. When this covenant is signed, it sets up the absolute chronology of the period between the signing of the covenant and the second coming of Christ as a period of seven years, quite in contrast to the indeterminancy of the length of the present age which will culminate in the rapture. Those living at that time, if they know the date when the covenant is signed, will be able to

foretell the approximate time of the return of the Lord
though still not able to fix the day or the hour.

Pretribulationists regard this seven-year period as being divided into two parts. In the first half, there is a
period of protection, one of comparative rest and tranquility
for Israel. They are protected from their enemies and
granted religious freedom. With the beginning of the second
half of the seven years, a period of persecution begins
when the covenant is broken. Israel is plunged into the time
of Jacob's trouble and the great tribulation of which the
Scriptures speak (Jeremiah 30:7; Daniel 12:1; Matthew
24:21; Revelation 6:17).

Pretribulationists view the end of the great tribulation
as culminating in the second coming of Christ, the deliverance of Israel, and the establishment of Christ's millennial
kingdom on earth. The great tribulation which precedes
the second coming of Christ is not only a time of persecution of Israel and of those who turn to Christ in that day
from both Jews and Gentiles, but it is a time of unprecedented divine judgments upon the earth which decimate
the human population of the earth and leave its physical
monuments and great cities in ruins. Interpreted literally,
the tribulation clearly eclipses anything that the world
has ever known by way of destruction of human life, great
earthquakes, pestilence, war, famine, and stars falling from
heaven. It is a time of trouble which leaves the earth in
shambles. It is indeed the day of God's wrath and righteous judgment upon a wicked earth. There will be multiplied thousands of martyrs, both of Jews and Gentiles,
who refuse to worship the beast and therefore suffer a
martyr's death.

The nature of the tribulation, if Scriptures relating to
it are interpreted normally and literally, gives no basis for
the idea that the church, the body of Christ, the saints of
this present age, will be forced to remain on earth through
it. According to the Scriptures, it is specifically the time
of Jacob's trouble (Jeremiah 30:7) and coincides with the

last seven years of Israel's program as outlined in Daniel
9:24-27. It is God's program for Israel, therefore, rather
than God's program for the church that is primarily in view.
It is also specifically the consummation of the times of the
Gentiles foreshadowed in Daniel's visions in Daniel 2 and
7, the progress of which was interrupted by the interposi-
tion of the present purpose of God in the church. The dual
purpose of God to fulfill Israel's program and the times of
the Gentiles culminating in the second coming of Christ are
quite different than His purpose for the church in this
present age. The church is composed of Jews and Gentiles
without distinction as to their racial origin and quite independent of God's program for either the Gentiles or
Israel as a nation. The fact is most significant that the
terms normally used of the church and which set it apart
as distinct from saints of previous ages are never found in
any tribulation passage. Though the argument from silence
is quite eloquent, in view of this complete absence of reference to the church as such, the burden of proof shifts to the
post-tribulationist to prove that the church is in this period.
That there is reference to Israel, to saints, to saved Israelites,
and to saved Gentiles does not prove that the church is in
this period as these terms are general terms, not specific.
Likewise, the term "elect" is not limited in any sense to
the church of this present age and, therefore, is not an
equivalent term.

Not only is the church not mentioned as being in the
tribulation time, but specific promises seem to be given to
the church that they will not enter this time of trouble. A
principal passage is found in I Thessalonians 5:9, previously discussed, where it is specifically said, "For God hath
not appointed us to wrath, but to obtain salvation by our
Lord Jesus Christ." The tribulation is definitely a time of
wrath (Revelation 6:17) and this appointment does not
belong to the church.

Confirming evidence is found in the promise given to
the church at Philadelphia in Revelation 3:10, "Because

thou hast kept the word of my patience, I will also keep thee
from the hour of temptation, which will come upon all the
world, to try them that dwell upon the earth." Whether or
not the church at Philadelphia is properly considered as
a type of the church as the body of Christ existing on earth
at the time of the rapture, it is evident that this promise
could not have been given to the church at Philadelphia
properly if, as a matter of fact, the church was destined to
go through the tribulation. The church at Philadelphia is
definitely promised that they will be kept out of "the hour
of temptation, which shall come upon all the earth" (Revelation 3:10). It is not as some have alleged that the church
will be kept through the tribulation, in other words, protected in this period. To the contrary, the Scriptures relating to the tribulation indicate that probably the majority
of saints in that period will not be protected, that is, they
will be martyred. Only a few, both Jews and Gentiles, will
escape the awful hatred of Satan and the world ruler. If
these passages pertaining to the tribulation are taken literally, the possibility of one who is identified as a believer in
Christ at its beginning, surviving to its end is indeed quite
remote. Probably the majority of those who survive the
period will be recent converts who come to Christ in the
awful time of great tribulation through the personal witness
of those who in many cases seal their testimony with their
own blood.

THE PRETRIBULATIONAL DOCTRINE OF IMMINENCY

One of the important arguments in favor of the pretribulational position is the fact that the rapture as presented in the Bible is constantly viewed as an imminent
event. In none of the major passages which predict the
translation of the living saints and the resurrection of the
dead in Christ are any events interposed as signs or indications of the approaching rapture. In such major passages
as John 14:1-3; I Thessalonians 4:13-18; and I Corinthians
15:51-58, the rapture is viewed as the immediate expecta-

tion of those who put their hope and trust in Christ. This is in sharp contrast to passages that deal with the second coming of Christ to the earth, such as Matthew 24-25, which outline a series of events that must necessarily precede His return and give special attention to the fact that the great tribulation must run its course first. The same view is outlined in great detail in the book of Revelation where the events portrayed from chapter 6 through chapter 18 must precede the coming of Christ pictured in Revelation chapter 19. It is impossible according to the pretribulationist to harmonize two such drastically different events as the coming of Christ for His church and His second coming to the earth attended as it is by all these important events preceding and following.

In like manner, the rapture doctrine is related to exhortations which lose much of their force if they are connected with the second coming of Christ following a great tribulation. In John 14:1 the introduction of the rapture truths in the upper room is prefaced by the exhortation, "Let not your heart be troubled" (John 14:1). In I Thessalonians 4:18 the rapture teaching is summarized in the exhortation, "Wherefore comfort one another with these words." Likewise in I Corinthians 15:51-58 the revelation concerning the translation of the living church is concluded with an exhortation to faithfulness and steadfastness in view of the fact that their labor is not in vain. In none of these passages are Christians warned that they must go through the great tribulation before they can see Christ coming for His own; and if such a contingency were in force, it certainly would remove much of the significance of these exhortations. The exhortation in I John 3:2, 3, is of similar character where the hope of the Lord's return is declared to be a purifying hope. Though a distant return of the Lord would also have some effect, it is clear that imminency makes much more urgent the need for present sanctification and purity of life.

Post-tribulationists often counter these arguments by

noting exhortations to "watch" and to be ready related to the second coming of Christ as for instance in Matthew 24-25. Here, however, the exhortation is clearly addressed to those who will be living in the period when the signs have already appeared. It is noteworthy that the exhortations are not given until the great tribulation is unfolded. It is therefore implicit in the passage that the exhortations do not apply specifically to those who are living in preceding generations, but rather have their immediate point in the lives and expectancy of those who go through the period of the signs related to the Lord's return. While they have general application to the entire interadvent age, their particular application is to those living at the time of the end.

THE HOLY SPIRIT IN RELATION TO THE TRIBULATION

In the discussion of the coming man of sin in II Thessalonians 2:1-12, a chronology seems to be set up which tends to confirm the pretribulational viewpoint. The Thessalonians, apparently misguided by a false letter, had thought that they were already in the time of trouble predicted for the end of the age. In correcting this misapprehension, the apostle assures them that it is impossible that they already should be in this period because certain things must occur first. He, therefore, exhorts them: "Let no man deceive you by any means: for that day shall not come, except there come a falling away first, and that man of sin be revealed, the son of perdition; who opposeth and exalteth himself above all that is called God, or that is worshipped; so that he as God sitteth in the temple of God, showing himself that he is God" (II Thessalonians 2:3, 4). He reminds them in II Thessalonians 2:5 that he had instructed them concerning this when he was with them at Thessalonica. He goes on to state further that they already know what is hindering the revelation of this person (II Thessalonians 2:6). The apostle then repeats what he had previously preached to them: "For the mystery of iniquity doth already work: only he who now letteth will let, until he be taken out of the way. And then shall that Wicked be revealed, whom the Lord shall consume with the spirit of his mouth, and shall destroy with the brightness of his coming: even him, whose coming is after the working of Satan with all power and signs and lying wonders, and with all deceivableness of unrighteousness in them that perish; because they received not the love of the truth, that they might be saved" (II Thessalonians 2:7-10).

This passage has given rise to a number of interpretations because it is not entirely clear what is meant by the restraint of iniquity. Probably the most popular interpretation is that this refers to human government which holds wickedness in check, and may refer specifically to the Roman government. Another suggestion has been made that true restraint of sin stems from God rather than man and what is referred to is the ministry of the Holy Spirit in this present age. In the upper room, the Lord had revealed to His disciples that He was going to send them the Holy Spirit (John 14:16, 17). The present age beginning with the Day of Pentecost has been called by many the dispensation of the Spirit. In this age there is an abundance of ministry of the Holy Spirit in the church in that every individual is indwelt by the Spirit, baptized into the body of Christ, sealed by the Spirit, and given new life by the Spirit.

The fact that the Holy Spirit came on the Day of Pentecost has suggested that the Holy Spirit will depart at the time of the rapture. This would be parallel to the coming of Christ who, though omnipresent in the Old Testament, came as a babe and dwelt among men for the period of His early life. Then He ascended into heaven and the state of things was restored to what had been before the incarnation as far as His personal presence is concerned. In like manner, the Holy Spirit came on the Day of Pentecost in a special sense, though He had been omnipresent for all eternity past. His special ministry having been completed in the

earth during this present age, He will then be taken out of
the world with the church and the situation will be restored
to that which was true before Pentecost. This seems to be
a reasonable approach and in keeping with numerous Scriptures bearing out the doctrine of the Holy Spirit.

The Holy Spirit is revealed to be the One who restrains
the manifestation of sin. Even in the period before the
flood, God had said, "My spirit shall not always strive with
men for that he is also flesh" (Genesis 6:3). The ministry
of the Spirit in the church not only ministers to the church
as such but constitutes a restraint of sin upon the whole
world. If the church is to be raptured as the pretribulationist holds, it would constitute a major removal of restraint
of sin.

In II Thessalonians 2, the restraining of sin is revealed
to continue until "he be taken out of the way." Only then
"shall that wicked be revealed," referring to the man of
sin of II Thessalonians 2:3. The person being removed is
a reference to that which restrains sin, namely, the Holy
Spirit of God. The chronology thus set up would be that
the Holy Spirit must be revealed first, then the man of
sin would be revealed and with it the falling away of the
apostasy in the time of tribulation. Inasmuch as the man of
sin is probably to be identified with the ruler of the revived
Roman Empire, his disclosure would come early in the
period and would presume that the rapture would precede
the beginning of the seven-year covenant which he makes
with Israel.

Another explanation has been offered in that the expression, "a falling away first," actually is a word meaning,
"departure." Some have taken this to refer to the rapture
itself, making verse 3 read, in effect, that the coming time
of trouble cannot come except there come a departure first,
namely, the rapture of the church. Though this interpretation has attracted the interest of pretribulationists, and
has some justification in usage, inasmuch as the text does not
explicitly indicate the departure of the church, it cannot

be proved positively that this is the correct view. Whatever evidence, however, is found in II Thessalonians 2 is in favor of the pretribulational position in that it seems to set up a chronology of events which places the rapture of the church first, to be followed by the revelation of the man of sin.

FULFILLMENT OF EVENTS BETWEEN THE RAPTURE AND THE SECOND COMING

The pretribulational view of the rapture of the church also allows for certain problems which are left unresolved in the post-tribulational position, namely, that a number of events seemingly follow the rapture and precede the second coming of Christ. The events on earth, of course, are those which characterize the tribulation period. Certain events, however, will also take place in heaven, namely, the judgment seat of Christ and the marriage of the Lamb. While these events would not constitute in themselves an insuperable problem to post-tribulationists, they fit so naturally in the pretribulational point of view that they constitute supporting evidence.

THE CONTRAST BETWEEN THE RAPTURE AND THE SECOND COMING

One of the most dramatic evidences for the pretribulational point of view is the sharp contrast between the revelation concerning the rapture and the revelation concerning Christ's return to the earth. In the major passages on the rapture such as John 14:1-3; I Thessalonians 4:13-18; and I Corinthians 15:51-58, the marvelous hope of the return of Christ for His own is unfolded. The revelation indicates that the event will take place in a moment and apparently that the earth and its inhabitants are left undisturbed. The Scripture does not use the term "secret rapture," and there is no sure evidence what the world will see and hear at the time of rapture. On the other hand, the Scriptures do not give any indication that the rapture will be subject to observation by the world as a whole. According to John 14:1-3, at the time of the rapture the church will be taken to the Father's house to the place prepared by Christ and the destiny of the saints will be heaven rather than earth.

The chief characteristics of the rapture accordingly may be summarized as including the factors that the saints will meet the Lord in the air, that living saints will be translated, that the dead in Christ will be raised, that the Lord will return to heaven with the saints, that the rapture will occur before the day of wrath, that it concerns only the saved, that it may be viewed throughout the church age as imminent, and that its promises relate only to the church.

A survey of the major Scriptures dealing with the second coming reveal an entirely different picture than the rapture. In Matthew 24, it is indicated that the second coming of Christ will fill the heavens with glory and will be "as lightning cometh out of the east and shineth even unto the west" (Matthew 24:27). Preceding the second coming in the tribulation time, the sun will be darkened, the moon will not shine, and the stars will fall from heaven. It is specifically predicted, "Then shall all the tribes of the earth mourn, and they shall see the Son of Man coming in the clouds of heaven with power and great glory" (Matthew 24:30). In contrast to the rapture, the second coming will be a visible event which both saved and unsaved will see.

A similar revelation is given in Revelation 19:11-16 where Christ is revealed to come from heaven on a white horse clothed with a vesture dipped in blood followed by the armies of heaven also on white horses and clothed in white linen. He is declared as coming with a sharp sword which proceeds out of His mouth with the purpose of ruling the nations with a rod of iron and inflicting "the fierceness and wrath of Almighty God" (Revelation 19:15). At His coming to the earth the armies of men which have

opposed Him are destroyed and the beast and the false
prophet are cast alive into the lake of fire. His return is
followed by His millennial kingdom.

In both of these major passages of Matthew 24 and
Revelation 19, no word whatever is mentioned of the rapture of the living saints. It is a time of judgment upon
a wicked world. Zechariah 14 indicates that His coming
will be to the Mount of Olives from which He had ascended
at the close of His earthly ministry and that when His feet
stand upon the Mount of Olives it will be divided in two
and a great valley will replace the present site of the
mountain (Zechariah 14:4).

There is little that is similar about the two events
except that both are referred to as a coming of Christ
from heaven to the earthly sphere. In contrast to the rapture, the second coming is a return to the Mount of Olives,
precedes the establishment of His kingdom, and is followed
by Christ remaining on earth for His earthly reign. It is
a time when sin is judged, it will follow the prophesied
signs such as the tribulation, and will deal with both saved
and unsaved. The second coming will affect not only men
but will result in Satan and his hosts being defeated and
Satan bound. In view of the decided contrast between
the coming of Christ at the rapture and His coming to establish His earthly kingdom, the burden of proof that these
are one and the same must rest with the post-tribulationist.
The facts would certainly point to the conclusion that these
are two events as different as any two comings of an individual could possibly be.

THE APOSTATE CHURCH OF THE TRIBULATION

Pretribulationists agree that while the church, the body
of Christ, is raptured before the tribulation, those in the professing church who are unsaved continue on the earth and
enter the tribulation time. They form the apostate church
of that period. The Scriptural revelation of this is found in
Revelation 17 where the apostate church is viewed as a

harlot and given the title, "MYSTERY, BABYLON THE GREAT, THE MOTHER OF HARLOTS AND ABOMINATIONS OF THE EARTH" (Revelation 17:5). Expositors of all classes have agreed that this is the apostate church of the tribulation time. It was customary in the Protestant Reformation to refer this specifically to the Roman Church and even modern expositors have had a tendency to return to this interpretation. It seems, however, that the apostate church is not only that of the remnants of the Roman Church but includes all Christendom as well as other religions, the whole united as a result of the trend toward a world church into a great superchurch. In the time of tribulation those who turn to Christ in faith remain outside this church rather than in it.

The apostate church is viewed as having evil association with the kings of the earth. The church will be in a dominant position as symbolized in the fact that she sits upon a scarlet colored beast which has seven heads and ten horns. This beast pictured earlier in the book of Revelation (Revelation 13) is to be identified with the revived Roman Empire. It is apparent that the revived Roman Empire and the apostate church work together to promote each other's power. The time comes, however, when the beast turns on the woman. According to Revelation 17:16; "The ten horns which thou sawest upon the beast, these shall hate the whore, and make her desolate and naked, and shall eat her flesh, and burn her with fire." This dramatic turn of events symbolizes the beginning of the great tribulation when the ruler who had previously dominated the Roman Empire rises to become the dictator over the entire world. Simultaneous with this assumption to political power, he demands that the whole world worship him (Revelation 13:8). As this conflicts with the demand of the world church, it becomes necessary to destroy the world church in favor of the new form of religion which will dominate the period of the great tribulation and be judged by Christ as His return.

Taking these factors into consideration, it is true in one sense that the church enters the time of the tribulation, but it is the apostate church composed entirely of those who are unsaved rather than the church, the body of Christ, which is raptured before these events take place. If the viewpoint of the pretribulationists be correct, the church will be in heaven during the time of the final struggle upon earth and will return with the Lord at the time of His second coming and will share with Him responsibility in the millennial kingdom. The prospect for those living in this generation who are in Christ is for His imminent return with all the blessings which this represents. For the world the sad prospect is that it will move into the end time with its unprecedented tribulation.

CHAPTER IX

THE CHURCH IN HEAVEN

After the rapture of the church, while the period of trial and trouble culminating in the great tribulation unfolds in the earth, the church is represented as being in heaven in the presence of the Lord. The Scriptures relating to this theme are supporting evidence for the pretribulation rapture inasmuch as the presence of the church in heaven is required in order to fulfill these prophecies. Scriptures relating to the church in heaven are occupied with two important themes: (1) the church as the bride of Christ in heaven; (2) the judgment seat of Christ. Of the various figures used to relate Christ to the church, the bridegroom and the church as the bride is the only one that is specifically futuristic and prophetic in character, contemplating as it does the future coming of Christ for His bride.

THE BRIDE OF CHRIST

The figure of marriage is often used in Scripture to represent spiritual reality. In the Old Testament, Israel is represented as the wife of Jehovah untrue to her marriage vows but destined to be restored in the future kingdom. In the New Testament, the church is presented as the bride of Christ not yet claimed by the bridegroom but waiting as a virgin for the coming marriage union. This concept is presented by Paul in II Corinthians 11:2, "For I am jealous over you with godly jealousy; for I have espoused you to one husband, that I may present you as a chaste virgin to Christ."

The use of the figure of a bride to represent the church in her relationship to Christ has in mind the oriental pat-

141

tern in which marriage is contemplated as having three major steps: (1) the legal marriage often consummated by the parents of the bride and the bridegroom in which the dowry is paid and the young couple are formally married in a legal sense; (2) subsequent to the legal marriage, the bridegroom according to the custom would go with his companions to the house of the bride to claim his bride for himself and to take her back to his own home; (3) the bridal procession would be followed by the marriage feast which would often last for many days as illustrated in the wedding at Cana (John 2). In the oriental marriage, there was no ceremony such as is common in western civilization, but the legal marriage was consummated by the parents in the absence of the bride and bridegroom.

Taking this figure as a spiritual picture of the relationship of Christ to His church, it is evident that for individual Christians, the marriage as far as its legal character is concerned is consummated at the moment an individual puts his trust in Jesus Christ as Saviour. In the case of the Christian, the dowry has already been paid in the sacrifice of Christ on the cross, and the bride has been purchased and claimed in a legal way by the Bridegroom. The church is, therefore, already married to Christ as far as the technical relationship is concerned. The day will come, however, when the Bridegroom will come for His bride and this is fulfilled in the rapture of the church. At that time the Bridegroom will claim His bride and take her to His Father's house. This is the background of the statements in John 14:2, 3 where Christ said: "In my Father's house are many mansions: if it were not so, I would have told you. I go to prepare a place for you. And if I go and prepare a place for you, I will come again, and receive you unto myself, that where I am, there ye may be also." This passage contemplates that Christ in the present age is preparing a place for His bride. When this is complete and the bride is ready, He will come to take the bride to her heavenly home which will be accomplished by the rapture and translation of the church.

Further light is cast upon this concept in the Scripture in Ephesians 5 in the exhortation to husbands to love their wives, "even as Christ also loved the church, and gave himself for it" (Ephesians 5:25). This, of course, refers to the death of Christ on the cross in which the price was paid and Christ demonstrated His love and made the necessary sacrifice. This past work of Christ is the foundation for His present undertaking presented in Ephesians 5:26 where Christ is represented as engaged in a work of preparation for His bride, "That he might sanctify and cleanse it with the washing of water by the word." The present work of Christ, therefore, relates to the sanctification of the church and her purification in preparation for the future marriage. This will be accomplished by "the washing of water by the word," best understood as referring to the teaching of the Holy Scriptures and their application to the hearts and lives of believers. The traditional view that this refers to water baptism is contradicted by the present tense of the verb. This is not an event, but a process, and one that continues throughout the life of the church on earth.

The ultimate purpose is stated in Ephesians 5:27, "That he might present it to himself a glorious church, not having spot, or wrinkle, or any such thing: but that it should be holy and without blemish." When Christ comes for His church, the transformation will be complete and the church will be a glorious church, that is, will reflect the perfections of Christ Himself. It will not have a spot, that is, any uncleanness or wrinkle, referring to the corruption of age in decay or anything of this character. Instead, the church will be holy, that is, perfectly conformed to the righteous standards of God, and without a blemish, i.e., without any natural disfiguration. In I John 3:2, the ultimate transformation is compared to being like Christ, "Beloved, now are we the sons of God, and it doth not yet appear what we shall be: but we know that, when he shall appear, we shall be like him; for we shall see him as he is."

The church which is made perfect by the grace of God will be delivered from the earthly scene and presented to the heavenly bridegroom on the occasion of the rapture of the church. The marriage union thus contemplated will result in the church being forever with the Lord (I Thessalonians 4:17), and it will fulfill Christ's declared purpose "that where I am, there ye may be also" (John 14:3). The Word of God pictures the relationship of Christ to His church as the most beautiful of love relationships in human experience and contemplates unbroken fellowship throughout all eternity as the church enjoys the immediate presence of their loving Lord.

Further confirmation is given that this is an event fulfilled in heaven rather than on earth in the millennium is the declaration in Revelation 19:7-9, at the time of the return of Christ to the earth to set up His earthly kingdom. The church is pictured as already the wife of the Lamb and as already arrayed in fine linen. The marriage of the Lamb is declared to have already come and now the invitation is extended to those outside the church, the body of Christ, to participate in the marriage supper (Revelation 19:9) which seems to be a spiritual representation of the millennium or at least its inauguration. As the marriage feast is the final stage, it should be clear that the Lamb has already come for His bride and claimed her previously in the rapture of the church. The marriage (Gr. *gamos*) is actually the entire ceremony subsequent to the coming of the bridegroom for the bride. In this marriage ceremony is the marriage supper (Gr. *deitnon*) which is the meal or supper proper.

The evidence taken as a whole confirms the pretribulational approach to this aspect of the future of the church and contemplates the consummation of the love relationship between Christ and the church in the symbol of holy marriage in heaven. The wedding feast which is the final stage is contemplated by some as occurring in heaven but is probably better related to the events which follow the second coming, especially in view of the fact that the announcement of the coming marriage supper is made at the very time that Christ is returning to the earth.

THE CHURCH REWARDED

One of the major features of the period during which the church is in heaven is the distribution of rewards for faithful service to the church at the judgment seat of Christ in II Corinthians 5:9-11. The fact of this judgment is declared to the Corinthian church: "Wherefore we labour, that, whether present or absent, we may be accepted of him, for we must all appear before the judgment seat of Christ; that every one may receive the things done in his body, according to that he hath done, whether it be good or bad. Knowing therefore the terror of the Lord, we persuade men; but we are made manifest unto God; and I trust also are made manifest in your consciences."

Here, as many other times in the Pauline letters, the church is challenged to labor for Christ in view of the necessity of ultimately giving account to the Lord after He comes for His own. It is a judgment which relates to Christians only and has to do with the matter of rewards for faithful service. Paul declares in II Corinthians 5:9 that this is a worthy motive for labor for Christ that "we may be accepted of him," or better translated, "that we may be well pleasing to him." The fact is stated that all Christians must appear before the judgment seat of Christ that they may receive a just recompense for what they have done in life. The basis of the judgment will be whether their deeds were good or bad.

It should be clear from the general doctrine of justification by faith and the fact that the believer is the object of the grace of God that this is not an occasion in which the believers are punished for their sins. All who are in Christ Jesus are declared to have "no condemnation" (Romans 8:1). It is a question of sorting out the good from the bad, the bad being discarded but the good being subject to reward. Paul mentions, however, in II Corinthians 5:11 that he is impelled by "the terror of the Lord" to continue in his task of persuading men to believe and serve the Lord. The terror which Paul mentions is not that of the possibility of being lost or unsaved, but rather the terror of coming before his Lord with a wasted life. In that day, when grace has brought him to the privileged place of being with the Lord in heaven, the thought of having to present a life that has not been properly spent in the Lord's service fills him with terror. It was this fear that drove him on in his service for the Lord.

The truth of the judgment seat of Christ, declared in its main principles in II Corinthians 5, is presented elsewhere in the Pauline letters under three different figures. One of the basic presentations is that of the believer's life as a stewardship. The child of God is pictured as having been entrusted with a responsibility which he must discharge on behalf of his master. On the basis of this stewardship, believers are exhorted not to judge others but rather to judge themselves. In Romans 14:10-12 this truth is presented, "But why dost thou judge thy brother? or why dost thou set at nought thy brother? for we shall all stand before the judgment seat of Christ. For it is written, As I live, saith the Lord, every knee shall bow to me, and every tongue shall confess to God. So then every one of us shall give account of himself to God."

Inasmuch as each believer must give account to God, it is presumptive for a believer to attempt to judge his brother especially in areas where doubt exists as to what the will of God may be. This does not mean that the preacher of the Gospel is not called upon to rebuke sin or to reprove those who are outside the will of God, but it does require a recognition of the fact that our judgment is not the final one. Ultimately our main question is not whether someone else is serving the Lord, but whether we ourselves are properly fulfilling God's stewardship as committed to us. The principle is plainly laid down, however, in verse 12, that everyone will have to account for his life at the judgment seat of Christ.

The thought of stewardship is reinforced and given further explanation in I Corinthians 4:1-5, "Let a man so account of us, as of the ministers of Christ, and stewards of the mysteries of God. Moreover it is required in stewards, that a man be found faithful. But with me it is a very small thing that I should be judged of you, or of man's judgment: yea, I judge not mine own self. For I know nothing by myself; yet am I not hereby justified: but he that judgeth me is the Lord. Therefore judge nothing before the time, until the Lord come, who both will bring to light the hidden things of darkness, and will make manifest the counsels of the hearts: and then shall every man have praise of God."

Here the Christian is especially reminded that he is a steward of the truth of God and that as such he is required to be found faithful. As in the Romans 14 passage, it is made clear that the main issue is not what man may think about it as there are limitations in our evaluation of our own life. Paul states that the Lord Himself is going to judge him and that therefore we should not attempt to evaluate our stewardship prior to that time. In judging the stewardship of a believer, God not only examines the act itself but the hidden motive and counsels of the heart which prompted it. Paul concludes with a note of expectation, "Then shall every man have praise of God."

A second important figure is used relative to the judgment seat of Christ in picturing the believer's life as a building built upon the foundation which is Christ. In I Corinthians 3:11-15, the foundation is described as already laid, which is Jesus Christ. Upon this foundation, each man is called to build a building or a life which will stand the test of God's final judgment. Paul writes the Corinthians: "Now if any man build upon this foundation gold, silver, precious stones, wood, hay, stubble; every man's work shall be made manifest: for the day shall declare it, because it shall be revealed by fire; and the fire shall try every man's work of what sort it is. If any man's work abide which he hath built thereupon, he shall receive a reward. If any man's work shall be burned, he shall suffer loss: but he himself shall be saved; yet so as by fire" (I Corinthians 3:12-15).

In using the figure of a building, attention is called first of all to the fact that it must be built on the proper foundation, namely, salvation in Christ. Everyone who appears at the judgment seat of Christ will meet this qualification as a person who has put his trust in Christ and has been accepted in the Beloved. Upon the foundation of our salvation in Christ, it is necessary for us to erect our lives. The materials mentioned are typical of what may be incorporated. The gold, silver, and precious stones represent that which is precious and indestructible, whereas the wood, hay, and stubble represent that which is unworthy and subject to destruction. As the passage makes plain, the building will be tested by fire and that which abides after it is tested by fire, namely, the gold, silver, and precious stones which by their nature are fireproof, are going to be made the basis for reward. Christians are assured, however, that even if their building be burned, they will be saved as far as their eternal destiny is concerned but they will be stripped of reward. This is stated in I Corinthians 3:15, "If any man's work shall be burned, he shall suffer loss: but he himself shall be saved; yet so as by fire." Comparing this to I Corinthians 4:15, it seems evident that every Christian will have something commendable about his life, but relatively speaking some will have a life mostly wasted, composed of wood, hay, and stubble, in contrast to those who have lived for eternal things as represented in gold, silver, and precious stones.

Many suggestions have been made concerning the typical meaning of these six building elements. The wood, hay, and stubble clearly represent three degrees of worthlessness as far as eternal values are concerned. Wood obviously is the best construction of the three and may represent temporary things in our life of a necessary nature as scaffolding in the construction of a building. However, when tested by fire the wood is destroyed even though it may be constructed well and be beautiful in its appearance. Hay represents that which is much more transitory, useful for animals but not fit for human consumption. Stubble represents that which is completely worthless. All alike, however, are reduced to ashes.

By contrast, the gold, silver, and precious stones, though much smaller in size and more difficult to obtain, are able to survive the fire. Gold in Scripture is typical of the glory of God and the perfection of His attributes and may represent that in our lives which is Christlike or which reveals the perfection of God's handiwork and grace. Silver is characteristically the metal of redemption and may speak of personal evangelism and of efforts in the extension of the Gospel. Precious stones are not identified and probably purposely are not related to any particular stone. This seems to refer to all other works of God manifest in the life of believers offering a great variety of beauty and color and illustrating that believers may serve the Lord in many different ways. The gold, silver, and precious stones, however, have this one important characteristic, that they are able to survive in the fire.

Taken as a whole, the figure of a building is a reminder, first, of the necessity of building upon Christ the foundation as the only true preparation for eternity. Second, our lives should be lived in such a way that they will have eternal value, and the time and effort extended will be worthy of reward by the Lord at the judgment seat of Christ. It is a reminder that the only real values in life are those which are eternal.

A third figure representing the issues raised at the judgment seat of Christ is used in I Corinthians 9:24-27 where the believer's life is compared to the running of a race or of contending in a fight. The apostle writes: "Know ye not that they which run in a race run all, but one receiveth the prize? So run, that ye may obtain. And every man that striveth for the mastery is temperate in all things. Now they do it to obtain a corruptible crown; but we an incorruptible. I therefore so run, not as uncertainly; so fight I, not as one that beateth the air: but I keep under my body, and bring it into subjection: lest that by any means, when I have preached to others, I myself should be a castaway."

According to this passage, the objective in running the race of life is to receive the prize from the Lord at the end of the race. We are to be guided in our life by this objective. Just as an athlete must apply self-discipline and be self-controlled in all areas in order to win the race, so also the Christian must make all things conform to the ultimate goal of pleasing the Lord at the judgment seat of Christ. Competing athletes, as Paul reminds us, do this to obtain a corruptible crown, that is, a crown of laurel leaves such as were commonly given at the races in Greece. By contrast, the Christian is looking forward to an incorruptible crown, that is, a crown which will not decay quickly like a crown of leaves.

With this incentive, the apostle declares that he himself runs not in an uncertain manner and that he fights not as one that is simply going through the motions. Instead he keeps under his body, literally, "beats it black and blue," thereby bringing it into subjection to his will. The apostle fears that having preached to others to dedicate their lives to the Lord and serve Him, he himself may be a castaway or one who is disapproved or disqualified. The reference to being disapproved does not relate to salvation, but to reward. It is a picture of an athlete who by breaking the rules is disqualified from winning the race. The figure makes plain that a Christian should bend all his efforts to living in such a way that he will not be ashamed when his life is reviewed at the judgment seat of Christ.

The concept of winning a crown or a victor's wreath at the end of the race is spoken of elsewhere in the Scriptures. In II Timothy 4:8, the Apostle Paul declares, "Henceforth there is laid up for me a crown of righteousness, which the Lord, the righteous judge, shall give me at that day: and not to me only, but unto all them also that love his appearing." Here the reward is viewed in a general way as recognizing Paul's righteous life at the judgment seat of Christ symbolized in the victor's crown. Paul does not claim to have a peculiar right to such recognition but declares instead that a similar crown will be given to all who love the appearing of Christ.

The eternal life which will be the possession of all true believers is likewise called a crown in James 1:12 and Revelation 2:10. James writes, "Blessed is the man that endureth temptation: for when he is tried, he shall receive the crown of life, which the Lord hath promised to them that love him" (James 1:12). This passage does not teach that some Christians will have life and others will not, but rather that the very possession of eternal life and its enjoyment in heaven is one of the forms of compensation which the believer will have for his life of service on earth, even though it is based upon the grace of God and the sacrifice of Christ rather than upon his own attainment. The same is true of the mention in Revelation 2:10 where the promise is given to the faithful martyrs, "I will give thee a crown of life." Those who suffer a martyr's death will all the more enjoy the freedom in glory of life in heaven which is their heritage.

The idea of a crown as a symbol of reward is also mentioned in I Peter 5:4 where the statement is made, "And when the chief Shepherd shall appear, ye shall receive a crown of glory that fadeth not away." The crown which is a symbol of reward is described here as a crown of glory that does not fade away, and in I Corinthians 9:25 it is mentioned as an incorruptible crown. It will be a glorious day for the saints when the Lord rewards His own.

Their recognition will not be transitory like the successes of this life, but will continue forever.

The various crowns mentioned in Scripture taken together are a symbolic representation of the recognition by Christ of the faithful service of those who put their trust in Him. II John 8 adds a word of exhortation, "Look to yourselves, that we lose not those things which we have wrought, but that we receive a full reward." While salvation is entirely by grace, rewards are related to faithfulness in Christian testimony and it is possible for the Christian to fall short of the reward that might have been his. Though there is a just recognition of attainment in faith and life, the saints in glory will nevertheless recognize that it is all of grace and that apart from redemption in Christ Jesus their works would have been unacceptable before God. This is brought out in the worship of the four and twenty elders in Revelation 4:10 who cast their crowns before the throne and say: "Thou art worthy, O Lord, to receive glory and honour and power: for thou hast created all things, and for thy pleasure they are and were created" (Revelation 4:11). If the four and twenty elders represent the church, as many believe, the fact that they are rewarded at this point in the book of Revelation is another indication that the church will be in glory following the rapture and translation while the tribulation unfolds in scenes of earth.

The final triumph of the church in relation to being in heaven with Christ will come at the time of His second coming to the earth when the church will accompany Him to the earth. Some find reference to this in I Thessalonians 3:13 in the phrase, "at the coming of our Lord Jesus Christ with all his saints." This phrase, however, may refer to the arrival of the church in heaven rather than the return of the church to the earth. More specific is Jude 14, where the prediction is recorded, "Behold, the Lord cometh with ten thousands of his saints." The church may well be numbered with the armies of heaven mentioned in Revelation 19:14 in the triumphal return of Christ to put down the wicked and to claim the earth which is rightfully His. In view of the imminent return of Christ, the prospect of the glory of the church in heaven is an ever-present one to saints of this generation, and the events which now are prophecy may become a reality very suddenly. Prophecies relating to the church in heaven, however, are only the beginning of a sequence of events which will carry the church into the eternal state.

Chapter X

THE CHURCH IN ETERNITY

Comparatively little is revealed concerning the church in eternity, but sufficient facts are given to provide at least an outline of the hope of the church. All conservative expositors agree that the church will have its place in the eternal state. Premillenarians also find the church associated with Christ in His reign on earth during the future millennium. Allusions to the state of the church both in the millennium and in eternity to follow indicate a blessed state for those who have entered by grace into the church, the body of Christ.

The Church to Be with Christ

One of the significant prophecies relating to the future state of the church is the fact that believers in this present age are promised to be "with Christ." In the preliminary announcement of the rapture of the church in John 14:3, Christ promised, "And if I go and prepare a place for you, I will come again, and receive you unto myself; that where I am, there ye may be also." Just as the church is promised to be with Christ in heaven in the period between the rapture and the second coming to the earth, so the church also accompanies Christ in a subsequent activity in the millennial reign and in the eternal state. Other Scriptures bear testimony to this same concept. In connection with the revelation of the rapture in I Thessalonians 4:17 the prediction is made, "Then we which are alive and remain shall be caught up together with them in the clouds, to meet the Lord in the air: and so shall we ever be with the Lord."

154

In the figure of the church as the body of Christ in Ephesians 5:25-33, the marriage figure itself indicates that the church will be with Christ even as a wife with her husband. Colossians 3:4 indicates, "When Christ, who is our life, shall appear, then shall ye also appear with him in glory." From these various passages and other allusions of similar nature, it may be concluded that the church will be in the immediate presence of the Saviour throughout eternity to come. The church is specifically mentioned as related to the second coming of Christ in Revelation 19:7-9 and is seen in the new Jerusalem in the eternal state as represented by the twelve apostles (Revelation 21:14).

THE CHURCH TO REIGN WITH CHRIST

In connection with the predictions concerning the future kingdom Christ told His disciples prior to His death and resurrection that they would join with Him in His kingdom and judge the twelve tribes of Israel. As recorded in Matthew 19:28, Christ said to His disciples, "Verily I say unto you, that ye which have followed me, in the regeneration when the Son of man shall sit in the throne of his glory, ye also shall sit upon twelve thrones, judging the twelve tribes of Israel." Further light is cast upon this in Paul's word to Timothy recorded in II Timothy 2:12, "If we suffer, we shall also reign with him." The fact that Christ promised His disciples that they would rule over the twelve tribes of Israel and promised to faithful members of the body of Christ a similar position of honor of reigning with Him, constitutes a confirmation of the premillennial concept that there will be an earthly kingdom between His second advent and the inauguration of the eternal state. These predictions imply a mediatorial kingdom in which Christ is the ruler and in which His followers will share responsibility. This, of course, is in keeping with the many predictions of the Old Testament.

In confirmation of this, Revelation 20 states that saints will join with Christ in His reign over the earth for one thousand years. This privilege is not only afforded the church but is also extended to saints who died in the great tribulation as martyrs. According to Revelation 20:4, John writes, "I saw the souls of them that were beheaded for the witness of Jesus, and for the word of God, and which had not worshipped the beast, neither his image, neither had received his mark upon their foreheads, or in their hands; and they lived and reigned with Christ a thousand years." These martyrs who are put to death by the beast in the time of the great tribulation just preceding the second coming of Christ are raised from the dead and participate in Christ's reign upon the earth. If this prediction is taken in its normal and literal sense, it teaches unmistakably that saints will reign with Christ and adds to previous revelation the fact that not only the church but also these noble souls will have part in the government of the millennial kingdom.

A further word is added in Revelation 20:6 where it is stated, "Blessed and holy is he that hath part in the first resurrection: on such the second death hath no power, but they shall be priests of God and of Christ, and shall reign with him a thousand years." This passage seems to go beyond previous predictions and includes all those who are in the first resurrection. From this sweeping prophecy, it appears that resurrected beings will have part in the government of the millennial earth and, though details are not given, it is evident that their resurrection is with a purpose that they may serve the Lord in this capacity.

Some dispensationalists have interpreted these passages as teaching that only the church, the body of Christ, has part in the millennial reign and that other resurrected saints will not have this privilege. This conclusion seems to be contradicted by Revelation 20:4-6. It is probably more accurate to say that the church will reign with Christ in a different sense than saints of other ages. An illustration is afforded in the book of Esther in the relationship of Esther and Mordecai to Ahasuerus. Esther, the queen, reigned with Ahasuerus as his wife and queen while Mordecai reigned with

Ahasuerus as his prime minister and chief administrative officer. Both Mordecai and Esther reigned with Ahasuerus but in different senses. It is possible that there may be a similar distinction observed in the millennial reign of Christ in that the church will follow her typical position as the bride of Christ while other saints will have other responsibility in the government of the millennium. There is no real need, however, for a sharp distinction between the church and saints, of other ages in the eternal state, though the Scriptures seem to indicate clearly that each group of saints will retain its identity throughout eternity.

THE RELATION OF RESURRECTED TO NON-RESURRECTED SAINTS

The Scriptures reveal that the citizens of the millennial kingdom will be formed of those who survive the tribulation and who are still in their natural bodies. These, composed of both Jews and Gentiles, will be occupied with normal life on earth and be the subjects of the millennial reign of Christ. They will plant crops, build houses, bear children (Isaiah 65:21-23), and in other ways have a normal life under the ideal circumstances of Christ's millennial reign.

The fact that these will still be in their natural bodies has raised a question as to the relationship of resurrected saints to those who are still living ordinary lives on earth. The problem has been magnified out of proportion by amillenarians who have attempted to show that a millennial reign of Christ is an impossibility.

It should be observed first that the relationship of spiritual beings with those in their natural bodies is not an abnormal or a strange one as illustrated in the present ministry of angels who are unseen and who do not have physical bodies. Angels do not have homes on earth and do not occupy themselves with ordinary affairs of life. Nevertheless, the Scriptures indicate that they are in the earthly scene even today and have part in the divine government and outworking of the providential will of God.

Further light is cast upon the relationship of resurrected beings to those still in their natural bodies in the post-resurrection ministry of Christ. Though this posed some unusual situations, such as Christ entering a room with the doors being shut and appearing and disappearing at will, there were actually no real complications. Christ was able to talk with His disciples and they were able to talk with Him. They were able to see Him and feel Him, and His presence was just as real in His resurrection body as it was prior to His death and resurrection. Though admittedly the complications of millions of resurrected beings is a larger one than that of one person as in the case of Christ, the fact that Christ was able to mingle freely with His disciples on earth makes clear that there is no inherent problem which cannot be solved by divine wisdom in such a situation. Here as in many other cases, the Bible does not stoop to our curiosity, but expects us to accept by faith that which the Scriptures reveal even though it is quite foreign to our ordinary experience. It is far more honoring to God to accept what His Word has indicated concerning the ministry of resurrected saints, even though it leaves some problems unsolved, than it is to challenge what the Scriptures reveal as impossible of belief. After all, it is entirely reasonable for Christ in His resurrection body to be King of kings and Lord of lords and head the government of an earthly situation such as is pictured in the millennium. It should not strain our faith to believe that other resurrected beings could share with Him in such a government. Some further light is cast on this problem, however, in the study of the Scripture revelation concerning the New Jerusalem.

THE CHURCH AND THE NEW JERUSALEM

In Revelation 21-22, a comprehensive prophecy is given concerning the New Jerusalem described as "the holy city, the New Jerusalem, coming down from God out of heaven, prepared as a bride adorned for her husband" (21:2). A wide variety of interpretation has been offered by expositors concerning the nature and significance of this revelation. Some have preferred to regard the New Jerusalem as purely a symbol and not actually conforming to the reality of a future physical city. Others, however, have preferred to consider the prophecy in somewhat a more literal sense as the dwelling place of the saints. They have differed only as to whether the main thrust of the passage is to describe a millennial situation or the eternal state.

From a comparison of the dimension and situation of the heavenly city of Jerusalem with the characteristics of the millennial earth in relation to the Holy Land, as for instance indicated in Ezekiel 40-48, it seems clear that there will be no city on earth such as the New Jerusalem during the millennial kingdom, as its dimensions far exceed the possibilities of placing it in the Holy Land.

It has been observed, however, that the New Jerusalem is not said to be created at the time of the end of the millennium and the beginning of the eternal state, but is rather described as coming down out of heaven as if it had been previously created and in existence for some time. Though the Scriptures are by no means clear on many of the important factors which would enter into such a decision, attention is called to the fact that, in John 14, Christ promised that He was going to heaven "to prepare a place for you." Some have interpreted this as being a specific reference to the creation of the New Jerusalem in heaven as the dwelling place of the saints.

If this interpretation be admitted, there is no particular reason why the New Jerusalem should not be in existence throughout the millennium and suspended above the earth as a satellite city. Though this is foreign to our present experience of material things, such a concept is not beyond the realm of possibility. If the heavenly Jerusalem is hovering over the earth during the millennial reign, it would be a natural dwelling-place not only for Christ Himself but for the saints for all ages who are resurrected or translated and therefore somewhat removed from ordinary earthly affairs. Their position thus close to the earth would permit them to carry on their functions in earth in connection with the millennial reign of Christ and yet would remove them as far as residence is concerned from continuing or mingling with those in their natural bodies and would solve the problem of lack of reference to a dwelling place for resurrected beings on earth during the millennium.

Though some have attempted to limit the inhabitants of the New Jerusalem to the church, the body of Christ, Scripture seems to indicate that while the church will be present, the saints of all ages will also be included. According to Hebrews 11:10, Abraham "looked for a city which hath foundations, whose builder and maker is God." Further, in regard to the saints of the Old Testament who died without receiving the promises fulfilled, it is stated, "They desire a better country, that is, an heavenly: wherefore God is not ashamed to be called their God: for he hath prepared for them a city" (Hebrews 11:16). Their hope of a city should not be confused with their hope of the land. The possession of the land promised to the nation Israel was to be realized by those still in their natural bodies who survived the tribulation and who were on earth at the time of the return of the Lord. The hope for the city, on the contrary, is for resurrected beings of the Old Testament as well as the New.

The inhabitants of the heavenly city are enumerated in Hebrews 12:22-24, "But ye are come unto Mount Sion, and unto the city of the living God, the heavenly Jerusalem, and to an innumerable company of angels, to the general assembly and church of the firstborn, which are written in heaven, and to God the Judge of all, and to the spirits of just men made perfect, and to Jesus the mediator of the new covenant, and to the blood of sprinkling, that speaketh better things than that of Abel."

Listed in the heavenly Jerusalem and included as its citizens are the angels, the church, God, Jesus, and the "spirits of just men made perfect." It would seem that this last phrase refers to the saints of the Old Testament as well as tribulation saints who with the church will form the resurrected company who will inhabit the heavenly Jerusalem during the millennium and the eternal state.

The New Jerusalem is given detailed revelation and is described in general "as a bride adorned for her husband" (Revelation 21:2). The figure of marriage is used for the church, for Israel, and here for the city in which the saints of all ages will dwell. The fact that the marriage figure is used for more than one entity in Scripture should not be considered confusing, nor should the city be identified specifically with the church. It is rather that the New Jerusalem has all the beauty and freshness of a bride adorned for her husband. In Revelation 21:3-8, it is revealed that the New Jerusalem will be a place of indescribable joy where there will be no tears, no death, no sorrow, no crying, nor pain. This is comprehended in the declaration of Revelation 21:5, "Behold, I make all things new."

In the further description of the New Jerusalem given unto John beginning in Revelation 21:9, John sees the city described as "that great city, the holy Jerusalem, descending out of heaven from God, having the glory of God." The general appearance of the city is described as that of bright light compared to a precious jewel with its major structure being of a clear substance "like a jasper stone, clear as crystal" (Revelation 21:11).

The Apostle John gives in considerable detail the dimensions of the city which is described as being foursquare with the length equal to the breadth and measuring 12,000 furlongs on each side and being a similar distance in height. The tremendous size of the city clearly eclipses anything known in human history, for 12,000 furlongs measure 1342 miles. Such a city would be larger in most dimensions than the Holy Land itself at its widest extent and clearly indicates that the city is not to be represented as being on earth in the millennial reign of Christ. Various suggestions have been made concerning the dimensions of the city, some viewing it as a tremendous cube, others as a pyramid, and still others as a sphere. In any case, the city is of sufficient size to provide a proper base of operation for the saints throughout all eternity.

Though the city may be suspended in space during the millennial kingdom, it seems clear from the narrative that with the beginning of the eternal state following the millennial reign of Christ, the heavenly city comes to rest upon the earth. This is substantiated by the description of the twelve foundations in Revelation 21:14 which contain the names of the Twelve Apostles of the land. Foundations intimate that the city will rest on them. Here the city recognizes the presence of the apostles representing the church, the body of Christ, and the fact that their names are inscribed upon the foundation symbolically indicates that the church itself is related to this heavenly city.

On the foundation the wall of the city rests, which is described as "a wall great and high" (21:12) having twelve gates, three on each side, with the wall itself measuring 144 cubits or over 200 feet in height (21:17). If these figures be understood in their literal sense, it would indicate that the wall is of sufficient height to constitute a genuine barrier to all who are not qualified to enter and at the same time is dwarfed by the size of the city inside the wall which is, of course, much higher. The gates have inscribed on them the names of the twelve tribes of Israel (21:12) which shows that not only the church, but Old Testament saints will be included in the heavenly city. The gates themselves are guarded by angels which is another confirmation that angels are included in the heavenly city as previously indicated in Hebrews 12:22.

A dazzling description is given of the beauty of this city and of its materials in Revelation 21:18-22. The wall itself is made of jasper previously described as like a beautiful jewel clear in color. The city as a whole is pictured as "pure gold, like unto clear glass." The gold of the heavenly city is different than the metal of gold common to our present life and may refer to the city being golden in color rather than composed of the precious metal. Whatever its substance, it is transparent and at the same time is gold in appearance.

The foundation of the wall of the city is decorated with twelve precious jewels described in Revelation 21:19, 20. These jewels represent every beautiful color of the rainbow and present an image of indescribable beauty fitting for this city which is the masterpiece of God's wisdom and power.

The twelve gates are said to be twelve pearls, each gate being composed of one gigantic pearl. The streets of the city in Revelation 21:21, like the city as a whole, are compared to pure gold transparent like glass.

In the subsequent description, various aspects of the city are mentioned. Revelation 21:22 mentions that there is no temple in the city in contrast to the temples of earth and the temple of the millennial kingdom. God Himself dwells in the city, and it is declared, "I saw no temple therein: for the Lord God Almighty and the Lamb are the temple of it." Because of the presence of God in the city, there is no need for natural light. According to Revelation 21:23, "The city had no need of the sun, neither of the moon, to shine in it: for the glory of God did lighten, and the lamb is the light thereof." This city will know no night (Revelation 21:25) being lighted by continued radiance of the glory and presence of God.

Into this city, according to Revelation 21:24, the nations of them which are saved shall walk and the kings of earth will bring their glory into it. The reference to "the nations," literally, "the Gentiles," indicates that in the eternal state the racial and spiritual background of different groups of saints will be respected and continued. Old Testament saints will still be classified as Old Testament saints, the church will still be the body of Christ, and Israelites will still be Israelites as well as Gentiles Gentiles. Just as there will be corporate identity, so will there be individual identity. The notion that all identities will be lost in eternity is not sustained by careful examination of this description of the eternal state.

The blessing of entering the city, however, is limited to the saints and it is plainly stated that no one who does not qualify by being written in the Lamb's book of life is permitted to enter the city. It is a gracious provision for those who are the objects of God's grace. Those who have spurned His grace in time will not know His grace in eternity.

In Revelation 22:1, a description is given of "a pure river of water of life, clear as crystal, proceeding out of the throne of God and of the Lamb." If the city be considered a pyramid and the throne of God at its top, the river can be pictured as wending its way from the top down to the lower levels. Though it is difficult to reconstruct the exact image that is intended by the Scripture, it is clear that this pure river of life, though it may be a real and material river, is nevertheless symbolic of the abundance of spiritual life which will characterize those who are living in the eternal state. In Revelation 22:2, it is revealed that there will be the tree of life in the heavenly city bearing twelve kinds of fruit, yielding fruit each month with its leaves providing for the health of the nations. The reference in the Authorized Version to "the healing of the nations" has been taken by some as proof that this refers to a millennial situation rather than the eternal state. In a proper translation, however, the word "healing" is rather "health" and implies that the leaves of the trees are for the well-being of the nations, but does not necessarily indicate that healing is involved. The whole context, referring as it seems to do to the eternal state, would seem to rule out any thought of necessity of healing in a physical way. This is confirmed by Revelation 22:3 where it is stated, "There shall be no more curse; but the throne of God and of the Lamb shall be in it; and his servants shall serve him." Their blessedness before His presence in that they will "see his face" and enjoy His presence is indicated as their possession throughout all eternity.

The revelation is concluded by the statement that the things herein revealed are about to come to pass and will proceed in logical succession subsequent to the return of Christ to the earth. In view of the blessedness of this situation, Revelation 22 concludes with the invitation, "And the Spirit and the bride say, Come. And let him that heareth say, Come. And let him that is athirst come. And whosoever will, let him take the water of life freely" (Revelation 22:17). John himself, as he contemplated the glory of the future, breathed a prayer, "Even so, come, Lord Jesus" (Revelation 22:20). Though many details are not revealed, the glory and wonderful prospect of the saints is given sufficient description to provide substance to our hope and a glorious expectation for all who put their trust in Christ.

Chapter XI

SIGNS OF THE APPROACHING END OF THE AGE

Prophecies as they relate to the church take on new significance when viewed from the world situation of the second half of the twentieth century. Though the rapture of the church is presented in Scripture as always imminent, that is, as possible at any moment, the present world situation provides many indications that the rapture itself may be very near.

Strictly speaking, there are no specific signs of the rapture, as Scriptures uniformly relate signs of the end of the age to events which will follow the rapture. If it can be demonstrated, however, that the present world situation is in fact a preparation for events which will follow the rapture, it may safely be concluded that the rapture itself may be very near. The signs of the approaching end of the age are not incidental or obscure factors in the current world situation, but rather stem from major events and situations which are comparatively recent. The combination of many such indications has tremendous significance, and it is safe to say that never before in the history of the church has there been more evidence that the end of the age is at hand.

THE REVIVAL OF ISRAEL

One of the most striking situations from the standpoint of Biblical prophecy in the current world situation is the remarkable revival of the nation Israel and their return to their ancient land. Students of prophecy, especially those who are premillenarian, have long recognized that God's program for Israel is one of the major revelations of Scripture. Beginning as it does with Abraham early in Genesis, its prophecies continue and have their culmination in the last book of the Bible, the book of Revelation. That God is beginning to move once again in the nation Israel after centuries of no apparent progress is a clear indication of the approaching end of the present age and the beginning of events which will bring history to consummation.

The revival of Israel and the formation of the new state of Israel on May 4, 1948, is set in the context of the growing importance of the Middle East. This area of the world which formed the cradle of human civilization as well as the setting of the early history of Israel is important for many considerations. The geographic location of the Holy Land is at the hub of three major continents, namely Europe, Asia, and Africa. It is indeed the middle of the earth and the center of God's dealings with the human race.

Because of the fact that the commerce of the world flows through the Mediterranean and the Suez Canal, the Middle East is of great importance economically and the nation that controls this area of the world is in a strategic economic location. Though for centuries this area has been poor in its economic wealth and development, modern events seem to have brought a shift in this respect and are indication that the Middle East will again become important in an economic way. This is illustrated by the economic development of Israel itself and the tremendous chemical and oil reserves which are found in that general area.

It has long been recognized that the Middle East is also important from a military standpoint. One of the primary objectives of both World War I and World War II was the control of the Mediterranean and the Middle East. It is obvious that any country which desires to play a major role in world affairs must have influence in this area, and every world conqueror has recognized the importance of the Middle East.

From a religious standpoint as well, the Middle East is important inasmuch as it is the cradle not only of Christianity, but of Judaism and of the Moslem faith. No area

of the world has been more important in its influence upon
subsequent culture, religion, and human thought than the
Middle East.

From a Biblical standpoint, the Middle East is most
important because it contains the land which was promised
to Israel. In the covenant which was originally given to
Abraham, he and his seed were promised the land as recorded in Genesis 12:7, "The LORD appeared unto Abram,
and said, Unto thy seed will I give this land." This promise
is subsequently repeated in Genesis 13:14, 15, and its exact
dimensions are outlined in Genesis 15:18-21, where it is
confirmed by a solid oath including the shedding of blood.
The promise of the land is further given an everlasting and
perpetual character in Genesis 17:8 where God said to
Abram: "I will give unto thee, and to thy seed after thee,
the land wherein thou art a stranger, all the land of Canaan,
for an everlasting possession; and I will be their God."

Abram died, however, without possessing the land and
the same was true of Isaac and Jacob. When famine over-
took the promised land, Jacob took advantage of Joseph's
invitation and with his family moved to Egypt. This was
a striking fulfillment of prophecy given to Abram many
years before in which God had predicted not only that the
children of Israel would go to a land which was not theirs,
but that afterwards they would come out with great wealth
and possess the Promised Land. This prophecy as recorded
in Genesis 15:13, 14, reads, "Know of a surety that thy seed
shall be a stranger in a land that is not theirs, and shall
serve them; and they shall afflict them four hundred years;
and also that nation, whom they shall serve, will I judge:
and afterward shall they come out with great substance."
Embedded in the promise of the land to Abram therefore
is the prediction of the first dispersion into Egypt and the
return of the children of Israel with great wealth to possess
the promised land. Both the sojourn in Egypt and the return
to the land were literally fulfilled as recorded in Exodus
and subsequent books of the Old Testament.

In return to the land, however, Israel failed to possess all of it, and, though for a time under Solomon much of the land was put under tribute, the prophecy of its ultimate and everlasting possession was never fulfilled in the Old Testament. Instead, after Solomon, the kingdom was divided into the kingdoms of Judah and Israel, and subsequently the people of Israel were carried off first in the Assyrian captivity in 721 B.C., and later in the Babylonian captivity beginning in 606 B.C. The prediction that they would be carried off into captivity because of their sins was the theme song of the prophets in the preceding generations and only after Israel failed to heed the Word of God was the promise fulfilled.

In the midst of the wreckage of Israel's culture and civilization, which included the burning of the city of Jerusalem and its beautiful Temple, Jeremiah nevertheless predicted that Israel would come back to the land after seventy years. According to Jeremiah 29:10, God promised that they would return to the land, "For thus saith the Lord, that after seventy years be accomplished at Babylon I will visit you, and perform my good word toward you, in causing you to return to this place." Both the promise that they would be carried off into captivity and that they would return to the land were literally fulfilled. In keeping with this, it is recorded in Daniel 9 that when Daniel contemplated the prophecy of Jeremiah which somehow came into his hands in a faraway Babylon, he set his face to pray to the Lord and asked the Lord to fulfill his promise (cf. Daniel 9:2 ff). In keeping with the prophecy and in answer to Daniel's prayer, Zerubbabel led 50,000 pilgrims back to their ancient land of Israel and subsequently the Temple was rebuilt and under Nehemiah years later the city and the wall were restored. Once again the principle of literal fulfillment of prophecy is illustrated in the fulfillment of prophecies concerning the captivity and the return of Israel to the land.

Not only were the dispersions into Egypt and into

Babylon and Assyria predicted, but according to Moses himself the sins of the children of Israel would result in their being scattered over the entire earth. According to Deuteronomy 28:63, 64 Moses warned the children of Israel, "And it shall come to pass, that as the LORD rejoiced over you to do you good, and to multiply you; so the LORD will rejoice over you to destroy you, and to bring you to nought; and ye shall be plucked from off the land whither thou goest to possess it. And the LORD shall scatter thee among all people, from the one end of the earth even unto the other; and there thou shalt serve other gods, which neither thou nor thy fathers have known, even wood and stone." The significance of this prophecy goes far beyond the other predictions in that in this revelation it states that the Lord would scatter the children of Israel "among all people." This was subsequently literally fulfilled following the rejection of Christ by Israel. In A.D. 70 the city of Jerusalem was destroyed, fulfilling Christ's own pronouncement in Matthew 24:2 and other references to the destruction of Jerusalem, and later the land of Israel was made desolate and the children of Israel scattered to the four winds. This condition of Israel scattered over the entire earth has continued for almost 1900 years and no significant reversal was witnessed until our generation.

Though dispersed among all the nations, the Word of God was miraculously fulfilled in that the nation Israel was nevertheless preserved. In keeping with Jeremiah's prophecy that Israel would continue as long as the sun and moon endure (Jeremiah 31:35, 36), Israel has been preserved as a distinct people in a situation in which any other race or nationality would have long since been swallowed up. Because of their distinctive religion, culture, and heritage, they longed to go back to their ancient land. In our generation the beginning of such a movement has already been witnessed. At the beginning of the twentieth century, there was not a single Jewish village in all of their ancient land and only approximately 25,000 Jews could be found scattered here and there in the area that once belonged to their forefathers.

The Zionist idea of a new state of Israel in the Middle East advanced by Theodor Herzl in 1897 began to take form only gradually. It received some encouragement when the Balfour Declaration was issued in 1917 indicating that the British government was favorable to the establishment of a homeland for Israel. This action, however, was nullified by the British government after World War I was over. By 1939, when World War II began, the number of Jews had increased in the Holy Land to approximately 400,000 and once again the idea of a Jewish state was looked on with favor. In spite of many betrayals and reversals, the new state of Israel was finally proclaimed May 14, 1948, and since that date has been a reality.

Though its first year was spent in war with its Arab neighbors and heroic measures were necessary for its survival, the state of Israel has made steady progress since, till now it is a well recognized and established nation among nations. Its economic development has astounded the world as land has been cleared, terraced, and irrigated, millions of trees planted, crops of all descriptions produced, as well as substantial industries. Large cities such as Tel Aviv and Haifa have sprung into being as well as the new city of Jerusalem as capital just west of the ancient city which is still outside the borders of Israel. Most important, however, is the fact that now approximately two million Israelites are back in their ancient land, constituting the biggest movement of the nation since the Exodus from Egypt some 3500 years ago.

From the standpoint of Biblical prophecy, the formation of the nation of Israel is of tremendous significance, for what is now being witnessed by the world seems clearly to be a fulfillment of prophecy that there was to be ultimately a complete and final regathering of Israel in connection with the second coming of Christ. According to Jeremiah 23:7, 8 Israel was to be completely regathered immediately after the return of Christ to reign on the earth. This prophecy states: "Therefore, behold, the days come, saith the LORD, that they shall no more say, the LORD liveth which brought up the children of Israel out of the land of Egypt; but, the LORD liveth, which brought up and which led the seed of the house of Israel out of the north country, and from all countries whither I had driven them; and they shall dwell in their own land." As the prophecy makes evident, the regathering in view here is distinct from all previous historic regatherings in that it is an assembly of the children of Israel from all the nations of the earth.

Further light is cast upon this in Ezekiel 39 where it is indicated that when the regathering of the children of Israel from all the earth is complete, not a single Israelite will be left scattered among the heathen. Ezekiel wrote, "Then shall they know that I am the LORD their God, which caused them to be led into captivity among the heathen: but I have gathered them unto their own land, and have left none of them any more there" (Ezekiel 39:28). It seems highly probable that the regathering of Israel, which has so significantly begun in the twentieth century, will have its consummation and completion after Christ comes back and all Israel is assembled in the Holy Land. This concept is repeated many times in the major and minor prophets and constitutes one of God's unfulfilled prophetic purposes.

Further light is cast upon this fulfillment in the prophecies of Amos 9:14, 15 which read, "And I will bring again the captivity of my people of Israel, and they shall build the waste cities, and inhabit them; and they shall plant vineyards, and drink the wine thereof; they shall also make gardens, and eat the fruit of them. And I will plant them upon their land, and they shall no more be pulled up out of their land which I have given them, saith the LORD thy God." In connection with this significant prophecy, it is noted that the children of Israel returning to their ancient land will build their waste cities, plant vineyards, and drink the wine, as well as make gardens and eat the fruit.

This is graphically being fulfilled already in the present restoration of Israel and will have future fulfillment also in the millennial kingdom. Of great significance, however, is the climax mentioned in verse 15 where it indicates that once God has regathered them and planted them on their land, "They shall no more be pulled up out of their land which I have given them, saith the LORD thy God." In contrast to the regathering from Egypt, which later was reversed in the Babylonian and Assyrian captivities, and the regathering from Babylon which again was subject to dispersal in the first century A.D., the final regathering from all nations is never going to be reversed, but the children of Israel will continue in their land throughout the millennial kingdom as long as this present earth lasts.

The force of these prophecies is illustrated by their literal fulfillment. The dispersion and regathering from Egypt was literal; the dispersion and regathering from Babylon was literal; the dispersion to the entire world is literal and the twentieth century is witnessing the beginning of the final literal return to the land. It is a proper conclusion that Israel back in the land is a preparation for the end of the age.

According to the interpretation followed by many premillenarians, Israel's consummation will involve a covenant for seven years with a Gentile ruler in the Mediterranean area. This covenant anticipated in Daniel 9:26, 27, is between "the prince that shall come" and the "many," referring to the people of Israel. It is transparent that in order for such a covenant to be fulfilled, the children of Israel had to be in their ancient land and had to be organized into a political unit suitable for such a covenant relationship. Prior to the twentieth century, such a situation did not exist and tended to support unbelief on the part of some that Israel would never go back to their ancient land and could never have such a covenant. The fact of Israel's return and establishment as a nation has given a sound basis for believing that this covenant will be literally fulfilled as anticipated in Daniel 9:27. If the rapture occurs before the signing of this covenant, as many premillennial scholars believe, it follows that the establishment of Israel in the land as a preparation for this covenant is a striking evidence that the rapture itself may be very near. Of the many signs indicating the end of the age, few are more dramatic and have a larger Scriptural foundation than the revival of Israel as a token of the end of the age.

THE RISE OF RUSSIA

One of the great phenomenons of the twentieth century has been the rise of Russia to a place of international power and importance in the mid-twentieth century. At the end of World War II, Russia was a broken nation with its major cities destroyed and the flower of its manpower lost in war. There seemed little likelihood at that time that within a few years Russia should be in a position to become a world power. In the years following World War II, however, just this has occurred. Though its ultimate military strength and potential may be debated, it is unquestionably true that the United States and Russia are today the most powerful nations of the world and that Russia is at the peak of its power in its entire history.

The rise of Russia is a significant factor in the end of the age due to prophecies that relate to an invasion of Israel from the far North. Two long chapters found in Ezekiel 38-39 are devoted to this prophecy. Though not identified with Russia by name, the prediction is given of an invasion of Israel in which the invading army is completely destroyed by an act of God. The time of the invasion is declared to be "in the latter years" or "in the latter days" (Ezekiel 38:8, 16) at a time when Israel has been regathered to their ancient land. Israel is described as dwelling in "unwalled villages" and "dwelling safely" (Ezekiel 38:11) after having been "gathered out of many people" (Ezekiel 38:8). The situation in Israel is pictured as one of rehabilitation of places formerly desolate in rebuilding of cities and the establishment of new wealth and power (Ezekiel 38:12, 13). Such a situation and battle does not fit any historic context, but with the return of Israel to the land in our modern day a condition is created which in many respects corresponds to the context of Ezekiel's passage.

One of the areas which Russia would very much like to possess is the Middle East with its tremendous reserve of oil and chemical deposits. The importance of the Middle East is growing in modern affairs and Russia probably desires this territory to the south more than territory in any other direction. An invasion of Israel in the twentieth century by Russia seems a likely development in the end of the age. The fact that Russia has risen to such power in our day sets up a situation which, coupled with Israel's return to the land, establishes the basic conditions set forth by Ezekiel for the fulfillment of its prophecy.

Though all the factors are not yet fulfilled and it can hardly be said that Israel is dwelling safely in their land at the present time, the rise of Russia coupled with the return of Israel to the land puts two major component parts together in a prophecy which would have been impossible of fulfillment prior to the twentieth century. The situation of Israel dwelling in unwalled villages is a modern situation, not true in the ancient past. Never during a period when Israel was in the land was Israel threatened by an army from the far North. Though the passage contains a number of unresolved problems such as the return to antiquated weapons and other details of the prophecy, the general picture unmistakably corresponds to the modern situation. The rise of Russia therefore is another factor in the contemporary situation in which the stage is being set for the final drama of the end of the age.

The Rise of Communism

Another important aspect of the rising power of Russia is a spectacle of the world-wide sweep of communism. Never before in history has a new ideology swept more people into its fold in less time than communism has accomplished since World War II. Approximately one billion people are under communistic government throughout the world and the penetration of communistic ideas in other lands is obvious.

The rise of communism is peculiar in many respects because never before in history has an atheistic philosophy gained such a wide footing in any generation. While in the past many nations were pagan and worshiped heathen deities and idols, it is unprecedented for a great nation such as Russia to embrace atheism as its official religion. The spread of atheism to China, as well as many other nations, has greatly enlarged its influence and future potential.

The significance of an atheistic system such as communism in the end of the age fits into the prophetic picture with remarkable precision. In Daniel 11:36-45, an absolute ruler is described who will "magnify himself above every God, and shall speak marvelous things against the God of gods" (Daniel 11:36). This king is represented as disregarding all the deities of his forefathers and exalting himself to a place of deity in their stead. In Daniel 11:38 he is further described as one who honors "the god of forces," literally, the god of military forces. This expression makes clear that this absolute ruler who regards himself as God is completely atheistic in his approach as reflected in his disregard of all deities and in his exaltation of military power as the only entity to be feared. It clearly identifies him with materialistic and atheistic philosophy. It would be difficult to define in simple terms the communistic philosophy more accurately than by the description, atheistic and materialistic, and as respecting only power in war. The false religion which will be epitomized in this ruler is therefore akin to communism in all its important principles.

According to Scripture, the false religion which this king forces upon the world is the final form of blasphemy and false religion which will characterize the world at the end time prior to Christ's return to establish His kingdom.

If this king is to be identified with the beast out of the sea of Revelation 13:1-10, as many expositors do, this ruler is the same as the one who was given power over the entire world and of whom it is predicted, "all that dwell upon the earth shall worship him" (Revelation 13:8).

The significance of communism, therefore, is that of a preparation or forerunner of this future false religion. Millions of young people in communist lands are methodically being trained that there is no God and are taught to respect only military power. Such a preparation is an obvious one for this future world ruler, and the communistic ideology, though not identical in some respects to this future false religion, is nevertheless its counterpart religiously and constitutes an evident preparation for the world-wide sweep of this false religion. The fact that communism has such a wide following today and has made such impressive gains in our generation is another major factor in preparing the world for its climatic end at the second coming of Christ. While Russia as a nation will never conquer the world, communism apparently will embrace all people except those who in that day turn to Christ.

THE GROWING POWER OF THE ORIENT

One of the important developments of the twentieth century is the rising power of Oriental countries such as Red China, Japan, and India. The release of these major countries from foreign domination and their growing importance from the military and economic standpoint has reversed a trend of many centuries. It is obvious that in future world affairs, the Orient will increase in importance. Its multiplied millions of souls, its large territorial area, and its potential for economic and political development are obvious to all observers.

From the standpoint of Biblical prophecy, the Orient is important because of certain prohecies which indicate its participation in events at the end of the age. In the Scriptures which describe the final world conflict, including a gigantic world war, one of the military forces is described as coming out of the East. The ruler of Daniel 11:36-45 is troubled by "tidings out of the east," apparently an indication of rebellion against him and military attacks from the East. This is given further light in the book of Revelation where in chapter 9 in connection with the sounding of the sixth trumpet an army is described as coming from the East from the great river Euphrates numbering 200 million and capable of slaying a third part of the earth's population (Revelation 9:15, 16). A later development of this matter is given prominence in the sixth vial of Revelation 16:12-16 where it is predicted that the Euphrates River will be dried up "that the way of the kings of the east might be prepared."

While many explanations have been given of this difficult prophecy, the most logical is that it refers to an army which comes from the East led by its rulers. Subsequent verses indicate that this army will proceed to the Holy Land and form a part of the military force to participate in "the battle of that great day of God Almighty" that will have its center at Armageddon which is properly identified as the Mount of Megiddo on the southwest rim of the valley of Esdraelon. This is the final great world battle which is under way at the very moment Christ comes back in power and glory to establish His earthly kingdom.

The evidence that a great army will come from the Orient and participate in the final world war conflict is a natural conclusion, and the extraordinary size of the army is in keeping with the tremendous population of this area of the world. The fact that the Orient is rising in power and in military significance in our day seems another development in keeping with the prophetic description of the end of the age and therefore constitutes a sign that the coming of the Lord may be near.

THE TREND TOWARD WORLD GOVERNMENT

One of the dramatic developments of the twentieth century is the rise of world government in the formation of the United Nations. Though students of political science have long dreamed of a world empire and conquerors of the past have hoped to achieve a rule over the entire earth, no government has been able to embrace the entire population of the world. The twentieth century, however, has witnessed the effort to unite nations in a form of world government with the purpose of averting international strife and warfare between nations.

The League of Nations which was formed after World War I proved to be premature, and without the support of the United States was soon doomed to failure. The rude reminder of World War II that war is not the best way to settle international government problems set the stage for a program which would provide a medium for discussion of international difficulties. Thus came into existence the United Nations following World War II which today embraces more than one hundred nations of the world and almost every prominent nation.

The rise of world government is especially significant from a prophetic standpoint because of plain Scriptures which predict that in the days immediately preceding the second coming of Christ a world government will be in operation. Early intimations of this are given in the prophecies of Daniel where in chapter 7:23 the final ruler and his empire is said to "devour the whole earth." The world government thus predicted is to be followed by the kingdom of Christ which will be brought into being at His second coming. Confirmation of this concept is found in Revelation 13, where the world ruler of that day is described as having power "over all kindreds, and tongues, and nations" (Revelation 13:7). This is obviously a government of far greater sway than any of the previous empires mentioned in Biblical prophecy such as that of Babylon, Media-Persia, Greece, or Rome. These empires, to be sure, embraced much of the civilized world but did not actually rule over "all kindreds, and tongues, and nations."

The significance of the formation of the United Nations

is probably not that of being an earlier stage of this world government. It is rather that the formation of the United Nations indicates an acceptance on the part of millions of people of the principle of world government as the only effective way toward world peace. Apart from Christians who entertain the hope of Christ coming as a means of bringing peace to the world, those outside the Christian faith have no alternative but to accept world government as the only way to peace. Millions of intelligent people today believe that the only hope of averting atomic suicide is to accept some form of international control in which individual nations will surrender some of their sovereignty in favor of international control. Though the rise of nationalism and independence of many small nations has for a time tended to fragmentize rather than unify the world, the weakness and interdependence of nations is even more apparent today than ever before. In a world brought close together by rapid means of travel and weapons of destruction which can reach any portion of the globe, the significant fact is that for the first time in history the concept of a world government has seized the minds of large masses of people. The world situation with its scientific improvements has developed to the point where such a world government becomes a necessity if future world conflicts should be avoided. The rise of the United Nations, therefore, is another apparent sign in progress toward preparation for the end in that millions of people are already prepared to accept such a world ruler when he rises in the last days. Trend toward centralization of power as manifested in all areas and as predicted for the end time is supported by the formation of the United Nations and its evident trend of increasing power in the world.

THE RISE OF THE WORLD CHURCH

The history of the church since apostolic times has been one of multiplication and division. Though a semblance of unity was achieved in the fourth and following centuries, division soon became characteristic of the church. The Eastern and Western churches divided in the eleventh century and further division took place in the Protestant Reformation. Within Protestantism itself, hundreds of denominations arose as well as thousands of independent churches. The process of further division and schism continued until the twentieth century.

In the last thirty-five years, however, a new development has come into being, namely, a trend back toward unification of the church. The desire for ecumenicity or a world church had long been discussed but did not take tangible form until preliminary meetings were held in 1925 and 1927. Out of this came the Temporary Ecumenical Council in 1938 and finally the World Council of Churches was formed in 1948. Since then, millions of church members have become party to a movement which is intended to bring together all branches of Christendom into one gigantic church including not only Protestantism, but the Roman Catholic and the Greek Orthodox branches.

From a prophetic standpoint, a world church of this character has unmistakable significance, because of predictions which anticipate just such a move at the end of the age. Apparently subsequent to the rapture of the church, a world church will emerge depicted in the uncomplimentary terms as a wicked woman in Revelation 17. This has long been held to represent a revival of the Roman Church and may well describe its course in a time when Protestantism and the Eastern church has rejoined Rome. Though all details are not supplied in the prophecy of this chapter, the woman who is labeled as "Babylon the Great" seems to represent the world church in the period immediately following the rapture of the body of Christ. The world church thus depicted will be superseded by the materialistic atheism which will characterize the great tribulation that will destroy the world church and replace it according to Revelation 17:16, 17.

The formation of a world church in the twentieth century from a prophetic standpoint, therefore seems to be a preparation for end-time events. The ecumenical movement as it is constituted today undoubtedly includes many genuine Christians. These, however, will be raptured at the time Christ comes for His own, leaving the organization bereft of any regenerated believers. Such a church will rapidly go into apostasy as the Scripture indicates, and prepare the way for the final form of blasphemy which will characterize the great tribulation.

While not a determinative sign in itself, the formation of a world church, added as it is to other signs that seem to speak of the end of the age, supports the concept that the rapture of the church may be very near.

The Trend toward Apostasy

One of the sad notes of prophecy as it relates to the end of the age is the prediction that instead of the church becoming better as the age progresses, it will grow worse and end in utter apostasy. As Paul wrote Timothy in II Timothy 3:13, "Evil men and seducers shall wax worse and worse, deceiving and being deceived." The extended passages of Scripture dealing with apostasy, such as I Timothy 4:1-3, II Timothy 3:1-13, and II Peter 2-3, combine in a testimony that the age will grow progressively farther from the truth and will justly deserve the judgment of God at its close.

Any observer of the theology of the contemporary church will recognize the drift which has been apparent in the twentieth century. A large portion of the church no longer subscribes to the inerrancy of Scripture, the eternity and deity of Christ, His substitutionary atonement, and His bodily return to the earth. These and other great doctrines of the faith have been rejected by the modern mind and replaced with a new theology. The present trend toward apostasy, according to the Scripture, is only the beginning and will have its ultimate form in the period after the church, the body of Christ, has been raptured. The presence of the true church in the world, containing as it does thousands of evangelical believers, has tended to stem the tide for the time being. But once believers are removed from the earth, there will be nothing to hinder the progress of false doctrine and the rejection of that which has characterized Christianity since its beginning. The change in the theology of the church is, therefore, another sign that the age is progressing to its prophesied climax and that the coming of the Lord may be very near.

When all the evidences relating to the end of the age as they exist in the contemporary scene are summed up, they contain an impressive list of events and situations which are peculiar to the twentieth century and especially to the post-World War II period. The revival of Israel, the rise of Russia, and the extensive power of communism, the growing power of the Orient, the development of world government, the formation of a world church, and the trend toward apostasy are major signs that the end of the present age may be very near. If so, prophecy as it relates to the church is headed for its consummation and the glorious promises which constitute the hope of the church may be fulfilled in the not too distant future. The devout soul, while striving to be "always abounding in the work of the Lord," with the Apostle John can sincerely breathe the prayer, "Even so, come, Lord Jesus" (Revelation 22:20).